More Than

A MONTH
OF
SUNDAES

KUDOS FOR
A MONTH OF SUNDAES

"First comprehensive history of the decadent dessert. As good as an ice cream sundae ripping with toppings." *-CBS Early Show*

"A Sundae Kind of Love–You'll find everything you ever wanted to know about sundaes, including the best parlors in the U.S." *-Playboy*

"Charming and informative." *-Amazon.com*

"Admiring Portrait of a Famous Temptation–weaves together sundae history, regional styles, folklore and recipes." *-New York Times*

"A charming, beautifully-illustrated book." *-Good Housekeeping*

"Full of mouthwatering wordplay." *-Arizona Republic*

"Sweet and breezy. . . ice cream lovers will lick their way through this book." *-MSNBC*

"It'll be a great summer with *A Month of Sundaes. -Booksense*

"Oozes with hot-fudge charm." *-Kansas City Star*

"Any Given Sundae–Who couldn't use this delicious book that scoops up recipes, large and small?" *-New York Post*

"Yum! A slurpingly delicious 30-chapter journey with easy recipes and lots of lore" *-Lifestyle Gazette*

"Nirvana awaits . . . irresistible and creamy-rich survey." *-The Boox Review*

"A dream book for ice cream fans." *-Times Herald*

"To get the scoop, get your hands on this book." *-Los Angles Daily News*

"Definitive history of the ice cream sundae." *-Book*

"Elegant, easy-to-follow recipes for all the components of a great sundae." *-Gastronomica*

More Than
A MONTH
OF
SUNDAES

by Michael Turback

RED ROCK PRESS

New York

MORE THAN A MONTH OF SUNDAES
by Michael Turback

ISBN: 1933176-2-4
Copyright © 2006 Michael Turback

Published by Red Rock Press
New York, New York
www.RedRockPress.com

Cover sundae photograph:
© Getty Images

Thank you to the following:

Barbara Leveroni, Franchise Associates, Inc., South Weymouth, Massachusetts,
for granting use of excerpts from Howard Johnson's Fountain Service Manual and
related materials.

Connie Berman of Media, Pennsylvania, for allowing use of the Hot Fudge Bagel
Supreme recipe, which appeared in Bagelmania by Connie Berman and Suzanne
Munshower, published in 1987 by HP Books.

Library of Congress Cataloging-in-Publication Data
Turback, Michael.
More than a month of sundaes / by Michael Turback– Updated ed.
p. cm.
ISBN 1-933176-02-4
1. Sundaes. I. Title.
TX795.T77 2006
641.8'62–dc22

2005029139

Book design by Kathy Herlihy Paoli, Inkstone Design
Manufactured in the U.S.A.

PRINTED IN THE UNITED STATES OF AMERICA

ACKNOWLEDGEMENTS

Whatever merit this book has is due in large part to the generosity of a great many people involved with the hospitality industry who freely gave me the benefit of their wisdom and recollection over the past five years. In particular, I would like to salute the following: "Ice Cream Joe" Greubel, Bryce Thomson, Joe Calderone, Monroe Udell and Kevin Donnellan.

I owe a particular debt to ice cream guru Steve Herrell of Herrell's in Boston for his willingness to take the time to share his expertise and enthusiasm with me.

I would like to thank my publisher and editor Ilene Barth, for suggesting this book, the Cornell Hotel School Library for its admirable research facilities, and Kathleen McCarthy for support and assistance.

Finally, I give my deepest appreciation to my wife, Juliet, for her encouragement and inspiration.

–MICHAEL TURBACK

PREFACE

History has a way of repeating itself. Perhaps a book about the ice cream sundae isn't crucial to the advancement of our democracy but as a home-grown invention, its study is more significant than one might suppose.

It was not until 2001, when I was commissioned by Red Rock Press to write *A Month of Sundaes*, that I fully recognized the attributes of this dessert that make it so original, enduring and authentically American.

To write about the ice cream sundae, I learned, is to consider the symbol of our abundance and appetite, our ingenuity, our never-lost youth. More than a book about a familiar dish, I believe that *Sundaes* also looks at American culture over time. Whatever twists and turns this country has taken, ice creams and sweet toppings have been standing by to lift our spirits. The sundae has interacted with our hard times, good times and odd times. In a nation of fickle tastes, it has shown remarkable durability.

Approaching the fourth anniversary of the publication of *A Month of Sundaes* (which was much applauded by culinary critics and other ice cream lovers, I'm happy to say), I decided it was time to take another look. When I'd finished revisiting soda-fountain culture, I'd added so much fresh material that my publisher decided the book deserved a new name. *More than a Month of Sundaes* delivers what it says. Like the cherry on top of our favorite concoction, the book now includes a 31st chapter–a guide to over 500 great places to find utopia in a dish. I hope you will enjoy this volume the way you might enjoy the second scoop in a double-dip sundae.

-Michael Turback, Ithaca, New York

TABLE OF CONTENTS

SPECIAL RECIPES

ere's a listing of recipes for selected top-quality sundae components. You may, of course, use store-bought premium ice creams
and toppings, instead. In its infinite variations and hearty helpings,
the sundae is an easy please, on any day.

ICE CREAMS

SAUCES & SYRUPS

OTHER TOPPINGS

SUNDAE BASES

Chapter 1

PURSUIT OF HAPPINESS

"In matters of principle, stand like a rock;
in matters of taste, swim with the current."

–THOMAS JEFFERSON

The happiness under consideration here rests on that most ephemeral of joys—ice cream. Chasing down the chef who first froze a dairy product is a pastime that leads to melting success. There are inklings that the concept may have been Himalayan or have originated in the robust appetites of ancient Rome, where the essence of a confection called melca appears to have been frozen milk. Long-ago Chinese emperors enjoyed a delicacy of iced milk and rice; Indians still prepare a cold dairy dish of antique origin called *kulfi*.

Marco Polo is said to have noted something resembling iced milk in his travels and so sparked adaptations in the royal kitchens of Italy. When the Italian princess, Catherine de Medicis, traveled to France in 1533 to marry the Duke of Orleans, she brought a recipe for ice cream along with her.

The English introduced ice cream to a new continent as they settled in America. Maryland governor William Bladen wrote of a dinner enjoyed in 1700, "We had a dessert no less curious; among the rarities of which it was composed was some fine ice cream." He pronounced the unfamiliar dessert "delicious."

The first recorded American verdict on ice cream was in.

Records kept by a New York City merchant show that George Washington ran up a $200 tab for ice cream during the summer of 1790, while serving as president in the nation's first capital. But Thomas Jefferson is the founding father to whom we most owe our gratitude for establishing ice cream as a national dessert.

Almost immediately upon his return to Virginia from his diplomatic post in Paris, French-style ice creams appear in visitor accounts of meals with the author of the Declaration of Independence and future president. One dinner guest described a menu that ended with "a very good ice cream—a dish somewhat like pudding, covered with cream sauce—very fine."

Another visitor observed: "Among other things, ice-creams were produced in the form of balls of the frozen material inclosed [sic] in covers of warm pastry, exhibiting a curious contrast, as if the ice had just been taken from the oven."

Ice cream scented with the heady aroma of vanilla was Jefferson's passion. His love of the spice was so fervent that, while serving as Secretary of State, he wrote to the American envoy in Paris complaining about a lack of vanilla in their fledgling nation, demanding that 50 plump vanilla bean pods be sent to him at once. This was a rather odd request considering it was at the height of the French Revolution, and heads were rolling.

Jefferson was able to enjoy ice cream throughout most of the year because ice was harvested from the Rivanna River in winter and carried to Monticello's icehouse, which held 62 wagonloads of it. The icehouse had double walls built with heavy timbers, the gaps between them packed with sawdust. The stone floors were carpeted with sawdust on top of straw, and allowed for proper drainage. Insulation was so efficient that in 1815,

HOME SWEET HOME

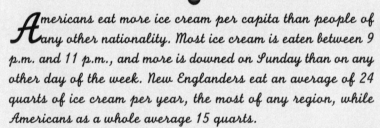

Americans eat more ice cream per capita than people of any other nationality. Most ice cream is eaten between 9 p.m. and 11 p.m., and more is downed on Sunday than on any other day of the week. New Englanders eat an average of 24 quarts of ice cream per year, the most of any region, while Americans as a whole average 15 quarts.

Ice cream is the comfort food preferred by both American men (27 percent) and women (23 percent). The good news is that ice cream, despite its fat content, has health benefits. Its calcium strengthens bones, its Vitamin A helps vision and its folic acid helps prevent birth defects. Eating ice cream produces brain chemicals like serotonin that elevate mood and lower blood pressure. It takes 50 bites to finish the average sundae, and that's a lot of pleasure.

Jefferson noted, his ice supply lasted all the way through mid-October.

During one particularly memorable dinner hosted at Monticello, guests were served his finest vanilla ice cream bathed in maple syrup and accompanied by meringue cookies. Such a treat exemplified one aspect of the "pursuit of happiness" Jefferson had championed for his countrymen. And ice cream topped with sweet sauce and decorated with wafers was a herald of the sundae yet to come.

THE RECIPES

FRENCH VANILLA BEAN ICE CREAM

*I*ce creams that use eggs are known as French-style ice creams or custards. What Thomas Jefferson would have loved about this extremely rich frozen custard is the flavor imparted by real vanilla bean pods and the thousands of tiny seeds that show up as little black specks. The seductively aromatic vanilla seeds infuse the ice cream with an elegant, sweet note soothing to the tongue and pleasing to the palate.

The most sophisticated vanillas are made with beans, not extract. The vanilla beans should be plump and pliable and feel dense and somewhat oily; the longer the bean, the better the flavor. My preferred contemporary version of Jeffersonian ice cream requires a paring knife to unlock the vanilla bean's flavor-intensifying power. Carefully slit open the vanilla bean pod from end to end to release the concentrated flavor of the seeds. Your reward will be a rich, complex and indulgent dessert.

You could try this classic French vanilla ice cream simply topped with pure maple syrup, to recreate the Jefferson party dessert, but I recommend adding warmth and crunch with maple-syrup bathed walnuts.

The guidance I offer assumes you are using an electric ice cream maker. But any of the ice cream recipes in these pages can also be made per manufacturer's instructions in a hand-cranked machine. It will just take more time and a lot more effort.

This recipe makes 1 1/2 quarts of ice cream.

3 large eggs	2 cups heavy cream
1 can (14 oz.) sweetened	2 cups half and half
condensed milk	Salt
1/4 cup brown sugar	1 vanilla bean pod

IN A LARGE MIXING BOWL, WHISK EGGS, CONDENSED MILK, BROWN SUGAR, HEAVY CREAM, HALF AND HALF AND A PINCH OF SALT. MIX THOROUGHLY AND TRANSFER TO LARGE SAUCEPAN. SPLIT ONE LONG VANILLA BEAN POD LENGTHWISE AND CHOP INTO 1-INCH PIECES, THEN ADD THEM TO THE SAUCEPAN. HEAT THE MIX TO A LOW SIMMER WHILE STIRRING CONSTANTLY, AND CONTINUE TO SIMMER FOR ABOUT 15 MINUTES. STRAIN INTO A LARGE BOWL SO THAT THE LARGER PIECES OF POD ARE LEFT BEHIND. ALLOW MIXTURE TO COOL AND AGE IN THE REFRIGERATOR FOR ABOUT FOUR HOURS; THEN YOU ARE READY TO MAKE ICE CREAM.

WITH MY ICE CREAM MACHINE THERE IS A MIXING BOWL, WHICH HAS A SMALL ELECTRIC MOTOR AND A PLASTIC DASHER. THE PLASTIC BOWL IS LINED WITH A METAL RING FILLED WITH A LIQUID THAT, WHEN FROZEN, HOLDS COLD THROUGHOUT THE ICE CREAM-MAKING PROCESS. I PREFER TO FREEZE THE MIXING BOWL OVERNIGHT IN MY REFRIGERATOR FREEZER.

JUST POUR IN THE MIXTURE, TURN ON THE MACHINE, AND 30 MINUTES LATER YOU WILL HAVE SOFT, CREAMY ICE CREAM. FOR SUNDAES, YOU WILL WANT THE ICE CREAM A BIT FIRMER. TRANSFER IT TO A CONTAINER AND PUT IT IN THE FREEZER FOR A FEW HOURS BEFORE SERVING.

WET WALNUTS

Toasting crisps the texture of the nuts and brings out their rich aroma and taste.

1 cup roughly chopped walnuts	1/4 cup light corn syrup
1/4 cup pure maple syrup	

PREHEAT OVEN TO 350 DEGREES. SPREAD WALNUT PIECES ON A BAKING PAN IN A SINGLE LAYER. TOAST UNTIL GOLDEN BROWN AND FRAGRANT, ABOUT 10 MINUTES. REMOVE PAN FROM OVEN AND SET ASIDE. COMBINE PURE MAPLE SYRUP, CORN SYRUP AND WALNUTS IN A BOWL, AND STIR UNTIL NUTS ARE WELL COATED. LADLE OVER THE ICE CREAM.

DUTCH CHOCOLATE
ICE CREAM

The dominance of the Dutch in cocoa trade and powder manufacture provided the primary ingredient for early chocolate ice creams. This recipe makes 1 $^1/_2$ quarts of ice cream with a rich, toasty flavor.

4 egg yolks	2 cups half and half
1 cup sugar	1 cup heavy cream
$^1/_3$ cup unsweetened cocoa	2 teaspoons real vanilla extract

WHISK EGG YOLKS. GRADUALLY ADD SUGAR, THEN COCOA, HALF AND HALF, HEAVY CREAM AND VANILLA EXTRACT, CONTINUALLY WHISKING UNTIL THOROUGHLY BLENDED. FREEZE, FOLLOWING THE DIRECTIONS OF YOUR ICE CREAM-MAKING MACHINE.

Chapter 2

FIRST LADY OF ICE CREAM

"Women in particular found so novel a taste irre-sistible, and nothing could be more amusing than their little grimaces they made when eating ice cream."

—JEAN ANTHELME BRILLAT-SAVARIN, THE PHYSIOLOGY OF TASTE

The great 20th-century chef and food writer James Beard laid America's love affair with ice cream at the feet of the country's second First Lady and first brilliant hostess. He credited Dolley Madison with starting our "long-lived ice cream binge."

Many founding mothers of America had little time for fashion, but Dolley seemed to have an intuitive gift for style. On the occasion of President Madison's second inaugural ball, the First Lady radiated from under a feathered turban. She wore a bright pink velvet flower-strewn creation with a square neck, and pink bows above a gathered, slit skirt, "the color of crushed

---

BRILLIANT PRESENTATION

Dolley Madison's White House kitchen used pewter molds for the extravagant ice cream creations she favored. Today, the St. Clair Ice Cream Company of South Norwalk, Connecticut, carries on the artisanal tradition of hand molded frozen desserts, reminiscent of a time when ice cream wasn't just served, it was presented. St. Clair's produces 17 ice cream or sorbet flavors in fruit, flower or other specialty shapes for some of the finer restaurants, hotels and caterers in the country.

SUNDAES CROSS THE POTOMAC

Originally part of the area surveyed for the nation's capital, the Potomac's west bank was returned to the Commonwealth of Virginia by the U.S. Congress and became Arlington. One of the city's most popular attractions is Lazy Sundae, an eclectic ice cream parlor, soda fountain and candy store. Servers fill an old-fashioned sundae goblet with house-made ice cream then top it off with thick hot fudge, a cloud of whipped cream, nuts and a cherry for Lazy Sundae's version of the Washington Monument.

strawberries," according to one observer.

Her magnificent costume was matched only by the highlight of her grand buffet table: a strawberry ice cream "bombe glace," molded to resemble Dolley's turban and of the same vivid pink as her gown. The dessert was made of cream from the Madisons' dairy, and strawberries fresh-picked from the garden of their Montpelier, Virginia, estate.

One guest described that great White House ice cream moment: "When the brilliant assemblage entered the dining room, they beheld a table laden with good things to eat, and in the center, high on a silver platter, a large, shining dome of pink ice cream."

Though slavery was still legal in the United States, two freed slaves were the creators of the ice creams served in the Madison White House. "Aunt" Sallie Shadd, who ran a catering business in Wilmington, Delaware, had developed the first recipes for artful, dome-molded, fresh-fruit frozen ice creams, and White House chef Augustus Jackson was responsible for perfecting the centerpiece ice creams served at Dolley Madison's soirees.

Jackson eventually left his position in the White House kitchen and moved to Philadelphia, where he started his own confectionery. The *Encyclopedia Britannica's Guide to Black History* refers to Jackson as the "Father of Ice Cream" for his use of ice mixed with salt to lower and control the temperature of the freezing mixture—a major breakthrough in the manufacture of ice cream as we know it today.

Chapter 3

PHILADELPHIA FREEDOM

"I doubt the world holds for anyone a more soul-stirring surprise than the first adventure with ice cream."

—HEYWOOD BROUN

arly American ice creams were made in pot freezers, also known by their French name, *sorbetières*. The ice cream mixture was placed in a bullet-shaped pewter pail, which was then set into a larger container holding four to six parts ice to one part rock salt, since salt lowers the freezing temperature of water. When salt is added to ice, the ice is forced to melt, drawing heat from its surroundings—in this case, the contents of the ice cream freezer. This chemical reaction cuts down appreciably on the time required for freezing.

The dessert maker churned and rocked the pail's outer container, stopping often to scrape the dairy mixture clinging to the interior sides of the pewter pot and stir it back in with a "spaddle," a miniature spade with a long handle.

Making ice cream of an appealing texture was a finicky and exhausting business. If the ice cream in progress was too soft, that meant the brine was not cold enough; more salt would be added to lower its temperature. If the ice cream was too coarse and icy, that indicated the brine had become cold too quickly; too much salt had been used. It took four to six hours of strong arm action and inside scraping and stirring to make one pot of ice cream.

The toil of ice-cream making was somewhat eased in 1846, thanks to an industrious Philadelphian named Nancy Johnson. Mrs. Johnson came up with a design for a hand-cranked tin freezer that "automated" the scraping and blending in its interior can. One operated her device by turning a topside crank connected to an S-shaped dasher in the freezer's interior drum. The dasher scraped ice crystals and kept the mixture in constant motion. This simultaneous freezing, scraping and stirring more efficiently incor-

STREETS OF PHILADELPHIA

In the later 1800s, ice cream was a street-side familiar. The most successful ice cream of the 19th century was made by William A. Breyer of Philadelphia. Since he couldn't afford to rent a store, Breyer hand-cranked ice creams in his kitchen and peddled them from a wagon pulled by his white horse named Peacock. In 1882, he was able to open an ice cream shop, followed by a wholesale manufacturing plant in 1896.

His sons, Frederick and Henry, incorporated the business, expanded it into Philadelphia's suburbs and beyond, and developed the corporate logo featuring a sweetbrier leaf. The Breyers used pure, natural ingredients, limiting their formulas to milk, cream, sugar and natural flavorings, but eschewing egg yolks. This was genuine, native Philadelphia ice cream; such no-egg ice creams became the American standard.

porated air into the cream mixture, producing a smooth ice cream. It also required less ice in its outer drum than had the pot freezer, quite a boon in the days when ice had to be cut from a frozen lake, pond or river, then hauled and conserved until sold or used.

Mrs. Johnson sold the patent for her churn to Williams & Company, a Philadelphia kitchen wholesaler, who in 1847 was selling $3 models as fast as they could make them. Whole families sociably gathered on porches around their ice-cream freezers, each person taking a turn at the crank.

HAND CRANKING ICE CREAM WAS HARD WORK.

Nancy Johnson's invention broke the class barrier, liberating ice cream from the dining rooms of Presidents and families who could afford servants and delivering it to the tables of common folks.

THE ICE CREAM MASTERMIND OF PITTSBURGH

Alfred Cralle, an African-American, worked with his father in the carpenter trade as a young man and became interested in mechanics. Later, he settled in Pittsburgh where he obtained a clerk's position at Markell Brothers' Drug Store. The store's fountain was where he devised a tool to mold and serve ice cream. Cralle held patent number 576,395 for the world's first ice cream scoop.

THE RECIPES

OLD TIME VANILLA ICE CREAM

I learned how to make some of the very best homemade ice creams from my friend, Steve "Doc" Wilson of Fayetteville, Arkansas. He is the author of *Homemade Ice Cream: The Whole Scoop*, and his personal museum includes an amazing collection of ice cream scoops, milk shake mixers, advertisements, toys, drive-in trays and other manner of ice cream stuff.

Doc believes that ice cream is good medicine for a world where nothing is certain. "Notice that when a cold, sweet, refreshing bit of ice cream melts in your mouth, all your concerns melt away with it," says Doc. "Life, for one brief moment, is sweet, tranquil, and all is right with the world." His vanilla takes me back to Publick's Drug Store in South River, New Jersey, and my earliest ice cream memory. (Doc's vanilla is also the basis of my strawberry ice cream.)

Sweetened condensed milk adds a rich and creamy texture, as well as a sweet flavor to this ice cream. This recipe makes 1 1/2 quarts of Old Time Vanilla.

2 eggs	2 cups heavy cream
1 can (14 ounces) sweetened condensed milk	2 cups half and half
$^1/_4$ cup sugar	Salt
$^1/_4$ cup brown sugar	2$^1/_2$ tablespoons pure vanilla extract

IN A LARGE MIXING BOWL, WHISK EGGS, ADD CONDENSED MILK AND WHISK TOGETHER UNTIL THOROUGHLY MIXED. ADD SUGAR AND BROWN SUGAR AND AGAIN MIX THOROUGHLY. THEN ADD HEAVY CREAM, HALF AND HALF, A PINCH OF SALT AND VANILLA EXTRACT. LET THE MIX CHILL IN THE REFRIGERATOR FOR ABOUT 4 HOURS, WHICH ALLOWS IT TO AGE. FREEZE, FOLLOWING THE DIRECTIONS OF YOUR ICE CREAM-MAKING MACHINE.

STRAWBERRY ICE CREAM

Use strawberries when they are fully ripe—electric pink, smooth and fruity—for this summer treat.

1$^1/_2$ quarts Old Time Vanilla (refrigerated for 4 hours)	$^1/_2$ cup sugar
2 pints fresh, ripe strawberries	$^1/_2$ lemon

CLEAN AND TOP THE STRAWBERRIES AND CUT THEM INTO BITE-SIZED PIECES. ADD SUGAR AND THE JUICE OF THE HALF LEMON. LET STRAWBERRIES MARINATE IN THE REFRIGERATOR OVERNIGHT OR AT LEAST 4 HOURS. WHEN THE OLD TIME VANILLA MIX HAS BEEN SUFFICIENTLY CHILLED AND IS READY FOR USE, STRAIN THE STRAWBERRIES, RESERVING THE JUICE. PLACE THE STRAWBERRIES IN THE FREEZER COMPARTMENT OF YOUR REFRIGERATOR. COMBINE THE STRAWBERRY SYRUP AND VANILLA CREAM. FREEZE THE ICE CREAM MIX, FOLLOWING THE RULES OF YOUR ICE CREAM MAKER. WHEN THE ICE CREAM IS ALMOST FROZEN, ADD THE STRAWBERRIES AND FINISH FREEZING.

REAL PHILADELPHIA VANILLA ICE CREAM

In the mid-19th century, the term "Philadelphia Ice Cream" began to be used to describe ice creams made from pure, natural ingredients but without eggs. This Philadelphia vanilla provides an uncomplicated foundation for sundae artistry. This recipe makes 1 quart of ice cream.

2 cups heavy cream	³/4 cup sugar
1 cup milk	1 teaspoon vanilla extract

IN A LARGE MIXING BOWL COMBINE THE INGREDIENTS UNTIL WELL BLENDED. FREEZE, FOLLOWING THE INSTRUCTIONS OF YOUR ICE CREAM MACHINE. (TO MAKE A FRUIT ICE CREAM, ADD ¹/₂ CUP OF COARSELY CHOPPED FRUIT DURING THE LAST FEW MINUTES OF FREEZING).

CLASSIC STRAWBERRY TOPPING

Strawberry syrup is best made when strawberries are in season. Use frozen berries only if you must. This gorgeous syrup, chilled or at room temperature and poured over vanilla ice cream, is irresistible. Just add freshly whipped cream, with a cherry (or a whole fresh strawberry) on top for a perfect sundae.

2 quarts fresh, sweet straw- berries	1 cup sugar (a little more if berries are tart)

WASH, STEM AND CRUSH BERRIES, USING A POTATO MASHER OR FORK, AND CRUST LIGHTLY WITH SUGAR. LET SET FOR AT LEAST AN HOUR TO ALLOW BERRIES TO MACERATE AND RELEASE THEIR JUICE. A LITTLE LONGER IS OKAY. TRANSFER SWEETENED BERRIES AND JUICE TO A LARGE, HEAVY SAUCEPAN AND CAREFULLY

BRING TO A SIMMER. COOK, STIRRING OFTEN, FOR ABOUT 12 TO 15 MINUTES OR UNTIL SLIGHTLY THICKENED.

Mr. Franklin's Neighborhood

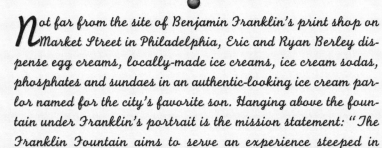

*N*ot far from the site of Benjamin Franklin's print shop on Market Street in Philadelphia, Eric and Ryan Berley dispense egg creams, locally-made ice creams, ice cream sodas, phosphates and sundaes in an authentic-looking ice cream parlor named for the city's favorite son. Hanging above the fountain under Franklin's portrait is the mission statement: "The Franklin Fountain aims to serve an experience steeped in ideals, drizzled with drollery, and sprinkled with the forgotten flavors of the American past."

THE LIGHTNING ROD

Place a brownie on a 6-inch plate. Dip one large scoop of coffee ice cream on top. Pour a double shot of espresso over the ice cream, sprinkle with chocolate-covered espresso beans and shredded coconut. Serve with a pretzel rod.

BROKEN HEARTS

Place a slice of brick vanilla ice cream on a 6-inch plate. Cover the ice cream with fresh, sweetened, and slightly crushed strawberries, and garnish with whipped cream; top off with two whole strawberries and serve with two Nabisco wafers.

–THE FRANKLIN FOUNTAIN, PHILADELPHIA, PENNSYLVANIA

Chapter 4

THE START OF SOMETHING BIGGER

"Invention, it must be humbly admitted, does not consist in creating out of the void, but out of chaos."

—MARY WOLLSTONECRAFT SHELLEY

Eighteen ninety-two was a year of invention. Ingenuity was everywhere. The internal combustion engine was invented that year. Mechanical lever voting machines were introduced. The zipper—introduced to fasten shoes—was patented. *Vogue* magazine debuted. James Naismith, a young physical education instructor at Springfield College in Massachusetts, nailed two peach baskets to the balcony at either end of a gym and came up with 13 rules for a new game called basketball.

Spectacular crime ruled the headlines: In Fall River, Massachusetts, Lizzie Borden dispatched her stepmother with an axe. Ninety minutes later, ditto her father.

But all was quiet in Ithaca, New York, a thriving college town at the southern tip of Cayuga Lake. Far above Cayuga's waters, Cornell University students rode those new "safety" bicycles, the ones with two wheels of the same size and air-filled tires. A popular stop was one of the neighborhood drug-store soda fountains, where many a nickel was spent for a dish of ice cream.

The Reverend John M. Scott delivered a sermon at the Unitarian Church one fine Sunday morning in April of 1892. That afternoon, he paid a visit to the Platt & Colt Pharmacy at 216

THE FIRST SUNDAE WAS ADVERTISED ON MAY 28, 1892 IN THE JOURNAL, ITHACA, N.Y.

East State Street, where ceiling fans whirred overhead while young men in white jackets dispensed potions from behind the marble top fountain. Proprietor Chester Platt, much to the delight of Reverend Scott, was about to scoop the competition.

Decades later, when the time and place of the invention of the sundae had become a matter of some dispute, DeForest Christiance, the Platt & Colt clerk who had witnessed the event, offered his testimony. Notice that Christiance does not claim credit for himself (making his version all the more credible) in the letter he wrote years later to Ithaca historian and librarian, John G. Brooks, describing the momentous occasion:

About the much discussed origin of the ice cream concoction called Sunday, Sundae and Sundi; About 45 years ago, on a Sunday afternoon, John M. Scott, then pastor of the Unitarian Church, and Chester Platt were having their usual Sunday confab in back of the prescription counter, when Mr. Platt proposed that they have some refreshment. Mr. Platt then came up to the soda fountain, where I was holding forth, asking for two dishes of ice cream, and on each he placed a candied cherry, then, after considering a bit, he poured cherry syrup over them, making a very attractive looking dessert.

When he and Mr. Scott tried out this new concoction, they became very enthusiastic about its flavor and appearance, and immediately started casting about for a suitable name. It was then that Mr. Scott said why not call it Cherry Sunday in commemoration of the day on which it was invented. This name appealed to Mr. Platt, so from that day on we served Cherry Sunday, and later on Strawberry, Pineapple, Chocolate, etc.

The new dessert soon became very popular with the student trade, so when they went home for their vacations they naturally told their local druggists about it, which soon spread the name throughout the country. It was only a short time afterward that one of the fruit syrup manufacturers came out with the name Sundae, and later a competitor spelled it Sundai or Sundi. The original, which I am satisfied was first prepared and named in the old Platt & Colt Pharmacy, was as you know spelled "Sunday."

–DeForest Christiance, May 25, 1936

SUNDAE READING

"*S*undaes cause acne," warned Humbert Humbert in Vladimir Nabokov's <u>Lolita</u>. Much of the great 20th-century novel, was written in Nabokov's apartment on East Seneca Street in Ithaca, New York.

As Christiance suggests, the young men and women who attended Cornell and hailed from all over the country created a buzz around the frozen novelty. As students returned home from school for summer vacations, they carried news of the "Sunday."

Platt, in his own right, showed a distinctly American knack for promotion. Besides the original concoction, he added a strawberry version to the menu, and both dishes were regularly advertised in the *Ithaca Journal*.

THE RECIPE

MEXICAN SUNDAE

Today, Purity Ice Cream is the pride of Ithaca, first in the hearts and stomachs of both natives and students. The ice cream company was opened in 1936, by Leo Guentert, a German immigrant who'd studied dairy science at Cornell before going to work for the Nestle Company, and then opening a business of his own. He named his start up Purity to reflect the strict hygienic standards he'd learned at Cornell. Salty nuts counterpoint the sweet chocolate syrup in Purity's Mexican Sundae.

DIP TWO LARGE SCOOPS OF VANILLA ICE CREAM INTO A LARGE SUNDAE GOBLET. COVER WITH CHOCOLATE SYRUP AND SPRINKLE A GENEROUS PORTION OF

SPANISH PEANUTS OVER THE TOP. GARNISH WITH WHIPPED CREAM AND PLACE
A MARASCHINO CHERRY AT THE TOP.

-Purity Ice Cream, Ithaca, New York

CHERRY ON TOP

The maraschino cherry originated in northern Italy where merchants added a liqueur to a local cherry variety called the __marasca__. By 1890, the delicacy was being imported into the United States, and was likely the candied cherry that appeared on the first sundae.

In 1896, U.S. cherry processors began experimenting, using a domestic sweet cherry called the Royal Anne, and substituting almond oil for the liqueur. By 1920, the American maraschino cherry was so popular that it had replaced the Italian variety in the United States.

Today, Gray & Company of Portland, Oregon, is the country's leading supplier of maraschino cherries with an 85% share of the market. The company ships six million cherries a day to groceries, bakeries, restaurants and scoop shops.

Chapter 5

GREAT PRETENDERS

*"The crushed strawberries of ice cream soda places,
the night winds in the cottonwoods and willows, the
lattice shadows of doorsteps and porches, these know
more of the story."*

—CARL SANDBURG

enry Louis Mencken, the cranky Baltimore newspaperman with a cigar perpetually jammed in the side of his mouth, hated the ice cream sundae. He called the "misspelled" dessert a "soda-fountain mess," and concluded that it was precisely the strange spelling that was responsible for its popularity.

Two Rivers, Wisconsin, a port city on Lake Michigan, is where Mencken placed the blame. In an essay published in 1922, Mencken recounted that a customer by the name of George Hallauer urged Edward C. Berners, owner of the town's ice cream parlor, to top a dish of ice cream with the chocolate sauce he used for ice cream sodas. Berners warned that it would ruin the ice

---

OLD TIME RELIGION

Evangelist Billy Sunday is noted as a major force behind the the adoption of Prohibition. One of his famous sermons, "Booze, or Get on the Water Wagon," convinced many people to give up drinking. Every year, his hometown of Winona Lake, Indiana, holds a Billy Sunday Festival featuring the Billy Sundae: three scoops of vanilla ice cream, a Twinkie, strawberry topping and whipped cream in a homemade waffle cone.

cream, but Hallauer ordered it anyway. The concoction caught on, but was offered only as a Sunday special. One weekday, a 10-year-old girl requested a dish of ice cream "with that stuff on top," asking Berners to "pretend it was Sunday."

If you didn't believe that story, Mencken had another one. In the nearby town of Manitowoc, George Giffy's best seller was plain vanilla ice cream, but when a customer pleaded with him to pour chocolate syrup, normally reserved for chocolate sodas, over a nickel portion of

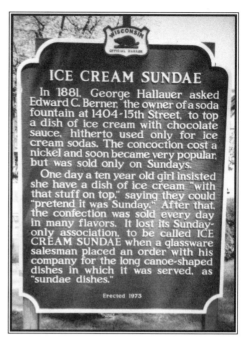

ICE CREAM SUNDAE MARKER IN TWO RIVERS, WI.

vanilla, Giffy realized he would have to charge an extra five cents to ensure a profit. The addition of syrup made the new treat too expensive to eat, except perhaps once a week—on Sunday—when dressed-up churchgoers filled his place. For the same strange motive that compels someone to misspell nightclub as "niteclub," Giffy changed the spelling to "Sundae."

Mencken was lampooning the insatiable American appetite for nonsense; he would admit that the tales cited above were something of a hoax.

Buffalo, New York, has its own delusion of historical grandeur. Their hometown legend traces back to Stoddard Brothers, the first drugstore to install a soda fountain in Buffalo, selling ice cream sodas for a nickel-until the day the store ran out of soda water. Uncle Charley Stoddard needed to dream up a new dish in a hurry, so he instructed his clerks to serve two scoops of ice cream drenched with fruit syrup. Charley's idea stuck, and so did the mythology.

Norfolk, Virginia, holds dear to its own unverified claim. A city ordinance not only prohibited the consumption of alcohol, but legislated against the growing "Sunday Soda Menace." To circumvent the blue law, it is purported that a local fountain owner added a few berries, fruit syrup and ice cream to an ice cream soda glass, but held off on the fizzy water. With a bit of legal subterfuge, his "dry" soda became a sundae.

BLESSED SUNDAE

In Origins, his etymological dictionary, Eric Partridge informs us that the ice cream sundae doubtless derives from the word, Sunday, because "an ordinary ice cream was good enough for a weekday, [but] only this special kind was good enough for a Sunday."

The assertion of Plainfield, Illinois, is, perhaps, least believable of all. It's said that in response to the urgings of his patrons, a Plainfield druggist dressed a dish of ice cream with syrup and decided to call it the "Sonntag" after his surname. *Sonntag* means Sunday in German, and you already know the rest.

While not making the same claim, Evanston, Illinois, does hold a dubious distinction in ice cream history. A devoutly Methodist town, Evanston not only banned saloons, it prohibited the sale of ice cream sodas on Sunday. After word spread from Ithaca about another "frilly" temptation, and this one (God forbid!) named after the Lord's day, religious lead-

A DRUGSTRORE FOUNTAIN, CIRCA 1900.

ers took to the pulpits. They struck fear in the hearts of local retailers, forcing a change in the spelling of "Sunday" to "sundae," thereby removing any connection to the Sabbath.

THE RECIPES

EASY CHOCOLATE ICE CREAM

This recipe can be made into double-chocolate ice cream by stirring in $^3/_4$ cup of semisweet chocolate mini-chips ten or fifteen minutes before ice cream freezing time is over. Makes one quart of ice cream.

2 cups heavy cream $^1/_2$ cup chocolate syrup
1 cup milk

IN A LARGE MIXING BOWL COMBINE THE INGREDIENTS IN THE ORDER LISTED UNTIL WELL BLENDED. FREEZE, FOLLOWING THE INSTRUCTIONS OF YOUR ICE CREAM MACHINE.

CLASSIC CHOCOLATE SYRUP

This brings back childhood memories of opening cans of Hershey's with those triangle can openers that pierce the top.

6 ounces semi-sweet chocolate $^1/_4$ cup water
$^1/_2$ cup evaporated milk

MELT CHOCOLATE IN TOP OF A DOUBLE BOILER. GRADUALLY STIR IN EVAPORATED MILK, AND CONTINUE STIRRING UNTIL SAUCE IS FULLY BLENDED AND SMOOTH. REMOVE FROM HEAT AND STIR IN WATER UNTIL SMOOTH.

SYRUP MAY BE REFRIGERATED IN AN AIRTIGHT CONTAINER FOR UP TO 3 WEEKS. TO REHEAT, SET OVER A DOUBLE BOILER AND STIR UNTIL SMOOTH. IF REHEATING OVER DIRECT HEAT, USE VERY LOW FLAME, AND BE CAREFUL NOT TO LET THE SAUCE BUBBLE OR BURN. MAKES 1 CUP.

WASHINGTON HOUSE SUNDAE

Two Rivers, Wisconsin, has created a replica of Ed Berners' Ice Cream Parlor in an historic boardinghouse, Washington House. Berners serves a patriotic sundae made with red, white and blue ice creams. The red is strawberry, the white is vanilla, and the blue is pistachio with a little help from food coloring.

DIP ONE LARGE SCOOP EACH OF STRAWBERRY, VANILLA, AND BLUE PISTACHIO INTO A TALL SUNDAE GOBLET LINED WITH CHOCOLATE SYRUP. COVER THE ICE CREAMS WITH CRUSHED STRAWBERRIES, CRUSHED PINEAPPLE, AND MARSHMALLOW SYRUP. GARNISH WITH WHIPPED CREAM, AND PLACE A MARASCHINO CHERRY AT THE TOP.

–Berners' Ice Cream Parlor, Two Rivers, Wisconsin

SCOTCH LASSIE

Beerntsen's of Manitowoc, Wisconsin, has been in the same family since 1932. Sundaes, made with Beernsten's own ice cream, include the Scotch Lassie.

DIP 2 LARGE SCOOPS OF VANILLA ICE CREAM INTO A WIDE SUNDAE DISH. COVER ONE SCOOP WITH BUTTERSCOTCH SYRUP AND THE OTHER WITH MARSHMALLOW CRÈME. SPRINKLE CRUSHED PECANS OVERALL, GARNISH WITH WHIPPED CREAM AND PLACE A MARASCHINO CHERRY AT THE TOP.

–Beernsten's Confectionary, Manitowoc, Wisconsin

MARSHMALLOW SUNDAE

Evanston ended its famous dry spell in 1972 and, besides beer and liquor, the good folks in this Chicago suburb now have the temptation of sundaes at Hartigan's.

DIP 2 LARGE SCOOPS OF CHOCOLATE ICE CREAM INTO A TALL GOBLET.

COVER WITH MARSHMALLOW CRÉME GARNISH WITH WHIPPED CREAM AND
PLACE A MARASCHINO CHERRY AT THE TOP.

-Hartigan's Ice Cream Shoppe, Evanston, Illinois

Chapter 6

SPLIT PERSONALITIES

"The Banana Republic chain is going to open stores catering to plus-size people. They're going to call it Banana Split Republic."

—JAY LENO

D avid Strickler, erstwhile proprietor of the Tassell Pharmacy in Latrobe, Pennsylvania, transformed the sundae into something even grander. During the summer of 1904, his dalliance with the tropical banana, sliced down the middle for easier eating, gave way to a flabbergasting fountain creation he called the banana split.

The new dessert was a symphony of delight. Three scoops of different-flavored ice creams were heaped on the sliced bananas; all was then enveloped by strawberries, raspberries and crushed pineapple. Strickler, the Toscanini of sundaes, added marshmallow syrup and chopped nuts. Finally, he perched a pitted black cherry atop each mound.

According to Strickler's son, William, it was his father's friend,

---

HOW TO EAT A BANANA SPLIT

F or Jim Powers of Kelly's Front Porch in Ocean City, Maryland, eating banana splits is a sensual ritual, a highly refined art. He describes the proper etiquette for feasting on one: "You always begin by eating the cherry, then discarding the stem. Move from one ice cream flavor to the next then back again. With each spoonful, try to capture ice cream along with the companion topping and a bit of banana. It takes a lot of practice, but it's worth it."

PHOTO BY TOM VANO.

Howard Dovey, who introduced the banana split to the world beyond
Latrobe. After working alongside the elder Strickler, Dovey left the pharmacy to attend medical school in Philadelphia, where he told fellow students
what the folks in Latrobe were eating. The students, in turn, encouraged soda
jerks in Philadelphia to embrace the spectacular new ice cream creation. By
the following summer, banana splits had reached the vacationer-thronged
boardwalk of Atlantic City, New Jersey.

Gus Napoulos was splitting bananas at the Elite Confectionery in
Davenport, Iowa, by 1906. Folks in Wilmington, Ohio, first ate Ernest
Hazard's banana and ice cream creation during the blustery winter of 1907,
and Letty Lally offered a version at the soda fountain of Foeller's Drug Store
in nearby Columbus that same year. In Boston, it was reported that an ice
cream entrepreneur started serving a similar dish with one minor flaw. He
served his banana splits with the skins on until he discovered that ladies preferred them peeled.

But it was an ambitious Chicago pharmacist who secured the banana
split's place in American culinary culture.

In 1901, Charles Walgreen borrowed $2,000 from his father for a down
payment on his first drugstore. After eight hardscrabble years, Walgreen sold
a half interest in his store to open a second location, where he installed a 16-
foot, marble-topped soda fountain, plus eight small tables and six booths.

Walgreen, who churned ice cream in the basement of this store,
dressed his clerks in crisp white uniforms with black bow ties to serve banana

splits in canoe-shaped dishes, and, as the chain of drugstores grew, soda jerks behind Walgreen fountains remained true to David Strickler's original. One exception occurred in 1926, when a young woman named Lucille Ball (yes, that Lucille Ball) lost her job at Walgreen's in Jamestown, New York. "I was fired," she told friends, "for forgetting to put the banana in a banana split!"

By the end of 1929, there were 397 Walgreens in 87 cities, and the banana split had become practically synonymous with the drugstore chain.

THE RECIPES

CLASSIC WHIPPED CREAM

To make the best whipped cream for sundaes and banana splits, use heavy cream with a butterfat content between 30% and 40%. The richer the cream, the more air it will trap and hold. Use a well-chilled bowl (I chill both bowl and beater in the freezer ahead of time). Most recipes call for confectioner's sugar, but I prefer to use sweetened condensed milk, which makes a more stable whipped cream.

1 cup heavy cream
¹/₄ cup sweetened condensed milk

COMBINE HEAVY WHIPPING CREAM AND CONDENSED MILK (BOTH WELL-CHILLED) IN A METAL MIXING BOWL. WHIP WITH A HAND-HELD ELECTRIC MIXER AT MEDIUM-HIGH SPEED. TO INCORPORATE THE MOST AIR, MOVE THE BEATERS UP, DOWN, AND AROUND THE SIDES OF THE BOWL DURING WHIPPING. WHEN THE CREAM HAS DOUBLED IN VOLUME AND FORMS STIFF PEAKS, YOU ARE READY TO ADD DRAMATIC SWIRLS TO A SUNDAE.

CARAMEL SYRUP

Caramel syrup, a byproduct of candy making, provides a zesty, tangy hot topping often used in banana splits or simpler sundaes.

1 cup granulated sugar	1 cup heavy cream
1/3 cup water	

COMBINE SUGAR AND WATER IN A HEAVY MEDIUM-SIZE SAUCEPAN. STIR CONSTANTLY OVER MEDIUM HEAT UNTIL SUGAR IS DISSOLVED AND THE MIXTURE COMES TO A BOIL. STOP STIRRING AND BOIL UNTIL THE MIXTURE TURNS A DEEP CARAMEL COLOR (TAKES 6 TO 12 MINUTES). WATCH CAREFULLY TO MAKE SURE MIXTURE DOESN'T GET TOO DARK.

REMOVE FROM HEAT AND ADD CREAM (CAUTION: MIXTURE WILL BUBBLE UP FIERCELY). RETURN PAN TO HIGH HEAT AND BOIL, STIRRING OCCASIONALLY, FOR 2 MINUTES. REMOVE FROM HEAT AND POUR INTO A GLASS MEASURING CUP OR OTHER HEATPROOF CONTAINER. ALLOW TO COOL TO DESIRED TEMPERATURE.

SYRUP CAN BE REFRIGERATED IN AN AIRTIGHT CONTAINER FOR UP TO THREE WEEKS. TO REHEAT, MICROWAVE ON LOW POWER AT 15-SECOND INTERVALS OR UNTIL WARM. MAKES 1 CUP.

FLUFFY MARSHMALLOW SAUCE

*R*ich and smooth, marshmallow provides an opposites-attract embellishment for chocolate ice cream.

2 large egg whites	16 regular marshmallows
1 cup sugar	1/4 teaspoon vanilla extract
1/2 cup water	

USING AN ELECTRIC MIXER, BEAT EGG WHITES IN A MIXING BOWL ON MEDIUM SPEED UNTIL SOFT PEAKS FORM (2 TO 3 MINUTES). SET ASIDE. COMBINE SUGAR AND WATER IN A MEDIUM-SIZE SAUCEPAN AND PLACE OVER MEDIUM HEAT. STIR UNTIL SUGAR DISSOLVES. STOP STIRRING AND ALLOW SUGAR/WATER MIXTURE TO COME TO A BOIL. BOIL FOR 3 MINUTES WITHOUT STIRRING. REDUCE HEAT TO LOW, ADD MARSHMALLOWS, AND STIR UNTIL THEY ARE COMPLETELY MELTED AND MIXTURE IS SMOOTH, ABOUT 4 MINUTES. REMOVE FROM HEAT AND, USING THE ELECTRIC MIXER ON LOW SPEED, BEAT HOT MARSHMALLOW MIXTURE INTO THE EGG WHITES. CONTINUE BEATING FOR 2 MINUTES. BEAT IN VANILLA. SERVE WARM OR COLD.

SAUCE MAY BE REFRIGERATED IN AN AIRTIGHT CONTAINER FOR UP TO THREE WEEKS. TO REHEAT, MICROWAVE ON LOW POWER FOR 30 SECONDS OR UNTIL WARM. MAKES 3 CUPS.

THE ROCKET

*I*nto a tall ice cream soda goblet place 1 scoop of chocolate ice cream and ladle on 2 ounces of chocolate syrup. Add 1 scoop of vanilla ice cream and ladle on 2 ounces of crushed pineapple. Then add 1 scoop of strawberry ice cream and ladle on 2 ounces of crushed strawberries. Split one banana lengthwise and cut the split halves again in half. Stick banana spears around the inside of the glass, pointed ends protruding over the top. Garnish with whipped cream and place a maraschino cherry at the top.

    –Edgar's at the *Pioneer Drug Store*, Elk Point, South Dakota

BANANA BLITZ

*P*lace 2 large scoops of vanilla ice cream on a banana split dish. Split one banana lengthwise and press halves against the sides of the ice cream. Dice a 3-inch-square brownie into small pieces and cover ice cream. Ladle on 2 ounces of hot fudge, garnish with whipped cream and place a maraschino cherry at the top.

    –Fair Oaks Pharmacy and Soda Fountain, South Pasadena, California

C.M.P. SPLIT

*P*lace one large scoop of vanilla and one large scoop of chocolate ice cream side by side on a banana split dish. Split one banana lengthwise and press halves against the sides of the ice creams. Ladle 2 ounces of chocolate syrup over the vanilla and 2 ounces of marshmallow cream over the chocolate. Sprinkle generously with salted peanuts.

    –Leiby's Ice Cream House, Tamaqua, Pennsylvania

Chapter 7

SOME LIKE IT HOT

"Always serve too much hot fudge sauce on hot fudge sundaes. It makes people overjoyed, and puts them in your debt."

—JUDITH OLNEY

ot many Americans recognize the name of Clarence Clifton Brown, but his accomplishment adds immeasurably to our popular culture. A restlessly curious man, Brown began dreaming about hot fudge sundaes back in 1906, when he opened an ice cream and candy shop in downtown Los Angeles.

His appearance was somewhat at odds with his profession. Hair parted debonairly in the middle, he resembled a banker more than a candy maker, a lawyer more than a soda jerk. With the prodigious energy that characterizes a great inventor, C.C. Brown labored every day in a kitchen at the back of his store, making candies and ice cream to sell up front. The secret of the liquid fudge he developed to pour over ice cream depended on subtleties and complexities in the blending of the sugars, not to mention the high boiling temperatures in his copper kettle. A less exact man would never have gotten it right.

Emboldened by success, in 1929 Brown moved the business to Hollywood Boulevard, a few doors down from Grauman's Chinese Theatre, where the footprints and handprints of movie stars are embedded in the concrete sidewalk. Ah, Hollywood! It's hard to imagine a location more suited to merchandising the epic hot fudge sundae. The store was designed in larger-than-life proportions, with glass double doors, huge candy display cases, a theatrical 30-foot high ceiling and a cinematic black-and-white interior. The perpetual motion

DOWN TO EARTH

🍒

*L*et the record note that when a U.S. astronaut returned from a three-and-a-half-month stint aboard Space Station Mir, NASA administrator Daniel Goldin's welcoming words were: "I'm saving a hot fudge sundae for you."

inside could very well have taken place on a studio set: nonstop ice cream dipping, frantic servers navigating the narrow aisles with trays of sundaes, and cash register bells ringing incessantly.

In the old days, Hollywood royalty, from Mary Pickford to Jack Lemmon, enjoyed C.C. Brown's sundaes in the high-back black walnut booths. Marlon Brando and his family were regulars in the 1960s. Brando, ensconced in his parked limousine, gobbled the addictive sundaes, while the rest of his family ate inside.

There was more than one way to eat a hot fudge sundae at C.C. Brown's. Your server scooped French vanilla ice cream into a silver-coated goblet then

C.C. BROWN'S OF HOLLYWOOD AT NIGHT.

added a dollop of unsweetened whipped cream and a sprinkling of chopped roasted almonds. Small brown ceramic pitchers filled with hot fudge were kept in a hot water bath until an order was placed, then served on the side. You could pour the sauce in one fell swoop over the top of your ice cream or parcel out the hot fudge over the course of eating your sundae. If you used just a little at a time, the fudge kept warmer, and there always seemed to be enough to insure that you wouldn't run out.

John A. Schumacher was a dairy chemist who had ventured west from Pennsylvania to work for the Carnation Company, then landed a position at C.C. Brown's. He adhered to a practice he'd acquired as a laboratory technician of dressing in white from head to toe. With his knowledge of candy making and loyalty to its traditions, Schumacher was the natural heir to the institution built by Brown. In 1958, he purchased the business from C.C. Brown Jr., and the Schumacher family extended the life of the legendary operation by another generation.

The seemingly endless summers ended in 1996 when the venerable sauce was poured over sundaes for the last time at C.C. Brown's.

THE RECIPES

CLASSIC HOT FUDGE SAUCE

Sundaes find expression in their sauces, and hot fudge provides a warm, flowing contrast in temperature and tone. For my hot fudge, the chocolate really must be in small bits or flakes to melt evenly. Use a candy thermometer for best results.

8 ounces unsweetened chocolate, grated or cut up fine
1/4 cup sweet butter
1 cup sugar

1 cup water
Pinch of salt
3 tablespoons light corn syrup
1/4 cup heavy cream

MELT CHOCOLATE AND BUTTER IN MICROWAVE OR IN A DOUBLE BOILER SET OVER HOT, SIMMERING WATER. IN A MEDIUM-SIZE HEAVY SAUCEPAN COMBINE SUGAR, WATER, CORN SYRUP AND SALT AND COOK OVER MEDIUM HEAT, STIRRING FREQUENTLY UNTIL THE SUGAR DISSOLVES—ABOUT 5 MINUTES. STOP STIR-

RING, BUT CONTINUE COOKING UNTIL MIXTURE REACHES 234 DEGREES ON A CANDY THERMOMETER—10 TO 15 MINUTES. REMOVE FROM HEAT AND STIR THIS SYRUP INTO THE CHOCOLATE AND BUTTER MIXTURE. WHISK IN THE CREAM.

IF NOT USING RIGHT AWAY, THE SAUCE MAY BE REFRIGERATED IN AN AIR-TIGHT CONTAINER AND KEPT FOR A MONTH. REHEAT OVER A DOUBLE BOILER, WHISKING VIGOROUSLY. IF REHEATING OVER DIRECT HEAT, USE VERY LOW FLAME, AND BE CAREFUL NOT TO LET THE SAUCE BUBBLE OR BURN. MAKES 2 CUPS.

JUST LIKE IN THE MOVIES— THE OREO SUNDAE

Forty miles from Hollywood is a soda fountain that looks like something right out of a Hollywood movie—literally. Key scenes for the movie, That Thing You Do, starring Tom Hanks, were shot at Watson Soda Fountain, a fixture in Orange, California, for a century. Since the look of Watson had not actually stood still, Hollywood set designers "restored" its soda fountain to the glory days of sundaes before on-location filming began. Afterwards, the drugstore kept its new "old" Hollywood fountain, serving old favorites, such as the Oreo Sundae which uses Oreo cookies to produce a soft yet crunchy square that's a cross between a cake and a cookie.

OREO BROWNIES

5 ounces unsweetened chocolate	2 teaspoons vanilla extract
¹/₂ cup unsalted butter, softened	¹/₂ cup all-purpose flour
1¹/₄ cups sugar	Pinch of salt
3 large eggs	12 Oreo cookies, coarsely chopped

PREHEAT OVEN TO 325 DEGREES. LINE A 10-INCH SQUARE BAKING PAN WITH ALUMINUM FOIL AND LIGHTLY OIL THE FOIL. PLACE CHOCOLATE IN A DOU-BLE BOILER AND MELT UNTIL SMOOTH (ABOUT 3 MINUTES). SET ASIDE BRIEFLY. USING AN ELECTRIC MIXER, BEAT BUTTER AND SUGAR IN LARGE BOWL UNTIL THE MIXTURE IS LIGHT AND FLUFFY (ABOUT 2 MINUTES). ADD EGGS, ONE AT A TIME, BEATING WELL AFTER EACH ADDITION. MIX IN MELTED CHOCOLATE AND VANIL-LA. ADD FLOUR AND SALT AND MIX ON LOW SPEED UNTIL COMBINED AND SMOOTH, ABOUT TWO MINUTES. WITH A RUBBER SPATULA, FOLD IN CHOPPED COOKIES. TRANSFER BATTER TO PREPARED PAN; SPREAD INTO AN EVEN LAYER WITH A RUBBER SPATULA. BAKE UNTIL A TOOTHPICK INSERTED IN THE CENTER COMES OUT CLEAN, 35-45 MINUTES. COOL ON WIRE RACK BEFORE CUTTING INTO NINE EQUAL PORTIONS.

SUNDAE ASSEMBLY

PLACE A 4-INCH SQUARE OREO BROWNIE AT THE CENTER OF A MEDIUM-SIZE PLATE. MORE THAN COVER WITH THREE SCOOPS OF VANILLA ICE CREAM, POUR HOT FUDGE SAUCE OVER THE ICE CREAM, TOP WITH WHIPPED CREAM AND SPRINKLE WITH CHOPPED PEANUTS.

– Watson Soda Fountain & Lunch Counter, Orange, California

ONLY IN AMERICA

*S*ome of the biggest venture capital deals in the Internet industry have been struck in a Silicon Valley institution called Buck's of Woodside, an eclectic café where you're greeted by a bright green Statue of Liberty holding aloft a giant hot fudge sundae.

Chapter 8

DOUBLE DIP DIVAS

"She was a butterscotch sundae of a woman."

—A. J. LIEBLING

The woman in question was Lillian Russell, a much-admired songbird in the early years of the 20th century. And her beauty was well matched by the words that flowed from A.J. Liebling, who was a food fancier (preferring simple food), a woman fancier (at least in his prose), and a life fancier extraordinaire. Liebling continued, "If a Western millionaire, one of the Hearst or Mackay kind, could have given an architect a carte blanche to design a woman, she would have looked like Lillian. She was San Simeon in corsets."

Lillian Russell required corsets, not only because it was her misfortune to be a lady in an era where fashionable woman sucked it in with a hoopla of string pulling and help from whalebone or facsimile stays, but also because she was lusciously *ample* in the way that worldly women used to be, which was also the way that men who loved them wanted them to be.

According to Oscar, who was the famed chef of the Waldorf Hotel, Lillian Russell ate more at dinner than Diamond Jim Brady, who was famous for his enormous appetite.

The Waldorf kitchen cut very cold cantaloupes into halves, removed the seeds, and filled the centers with vanilla ice cream. Garnished with whipped cream pressed through a small star tube, it was Miss Russell's favorite dessert.

In retrospect, we'd probably call Australian diva Nellie Melba "a peach of a woman," so attached has her last name become to vanilla ice cream matched with poached peaches in a raspberry swirl. But before Nellie was a sundae, she was a popular coloratura soprano, adored by Gay Nineties critics and fans. George Bernard Shaw wrote that Melba at her best sang with a "superhuman beauty."

Nellie attributed her success to her perfectionism. Hearing another rave review, she'd shrug and say, "If I'd been a maid, I'd have been the best maid in Australia. It's got to be perfection for me." She often happily declared, "I'm a snob!" Those who knew her best endorsed the sentiment.

Melba waged a battle with her weight. She believed one of the best ways of reducing was to roll back and forth on the floor, and she favored this exercise regardless of what she was wearing. Once she was observed rolling on the floor in a Parisian silk gown.

Inevitably, Dame Nellie's sparkling path crossed that of another perfectionist. Her equal in artistry was the French chef Auguste Escoffier, who brilliantly ruled over the kitchen and tables of London's Savoy Hotel. Escoffier's passions extended beyond the Savoy to the Royal Opera House at Covent Garden, where he, too, worshipped Nellie Melba, who often dined at the Savoy. On a spring evening in 1893, he attended a production of Wagner's *Lohengrin*. Nellie's performance as Elsa enchanted him and he determined to thank her by creating a dish to commemorate the occasion.

The next day, Melba arrived for luncheon, carrying her enamel-handled parasol studded with tiny diamond flowers and gold leaves. She ordered the plover's eggs *en croute* with fresh caviar and washed it down with champagne.

When it came time for dessert, Escoffier entered the dining room carrying a silver bowl nestled between the wings of a beautiful ice-carved swan—inspired by the majestic swan that appears in *Lohengrin*'s first act. The bowl held poached peaches on a bed of vanilla ice cream, covered with a lace of spun sugar.

Years later, at the opening of the Carlton Hotel in London, Escoffier decided to refine the dessert with the addition of a puree of raspberries and a sprinkling of sliced almonds. His composition was one of balance, nuance

FROZEN IN SNOBBERY

In the period-piece film, <u>Tea with Mussolini</u>, Maggie Smith portrays Lady Hester Random, a quintessential English snob. Anything that doesn't conform to her notion of propriety becomes subject to her scorn. Observing a sundae being served, she sniffs that Americans have even found a way to "vulgarize ice cream."

and jubilant deliciousness. Peach Melba is the name of the elegant sundae he'd created for a grand dame whose name thereby lives on even for those who've near heard an operatic note.

Escoffier was appalled at the liberty with which others interpreted his Peach Melba, replacing the raspberry purée with strawberry jam or currant jelly, or decorating the peaches with whipped cream. "The results obtained," he insisted, "have absolutely nothing to do with the original recipe and could hardly satisfy the palate of a real connoisseur."

THE RECIPES

CLASSIC BUTTERSCOTCH SAUCE

This old-fashioned hard-candy flavor has been a great sundae topping for a century. It's always best served warm.

1¹/₂ cups packed dark brown sugar	1¹/₂ cups heavy cream
³/₄ cup water	1 teaspoon pure vanilla extract

STIR BROWN SUGAR AND WATER TOGETHER IN A LARGE, HEAVY SAUCEPAN. BRING TO A BOIL OVER HIGH HEAT. REDUCE HEAT TO MEDIUM AND COOK FOR 2 TO 3 MINUTES AT A FULL BOIL, STIRRING OCCASIONALLY, UNTIL IT HAS THICKENED SLIGHTLY. REMOVE FROM HEAT.

WHISK IN CREAM AND THEN RETURN TO A BOIL, WHISKING CONSTANTLY. ONCE THE MIXTURE IS BOILING, WHISK ONLY OCCASIONALLY AND COOK FOR 5 MINUTES OVER HIGH HEAT, LOWERING HEAT SLIGHTLY IF THE SAUCE BUBBLES TOO HIGH AND THREATENS TO BOIL OVER. REMOVE FROM HEAT AND WHISK IN VANILLA. ALLOW TO COOL SLIGHTLY (MIXTURE WILL BE VERY HOT). SERVE WARM.

SAUCE CAN BE REFRIGERATED IN AN AIRTIGHT CONTAINER FOR UP TO THREE WEEKS. TO REHEAT, MICROWAVE AT 15-SECOND INTERVALS UNTIL WARM. MAKES 2 CUPS.

POUND CAKE MELBA

4 slices pound cake
Vanilla ice cream
4 poached peach halves*

²/₃ cup Melba sauce
¹/₂ cup toasted almonds, chopped

PLACE MATURE, PERFECTLY RIPENED PEACHES IN BOILING WATER FOR 2 SECONDS, REMOVE WITH A SLOTTED SPOON, AND PLACE THEM IN ICE WATER FOR A FEW SECONDS. PEEL, HALVE AND PIT THEM; SPRINKLE WITH A LITTLE SUGAR AND REFRIGERATE.

PLACE A SLICE OF POUND CAKE IN THE BOTTOM OF EACH OF FOUR DESSERT BOWLS. TOP EACH WITH A SCOOP OF VANILLA ICE CREAM AND THEN A PEACH HALF, CUT SIDE DOWN, ON THE ICE CREAM. LADLE MELBA SAUCE OVER THE TOP AND SPRINKLE WITH CHOPPED, TOASTED ALMONDS. SERVES 4.

MELBA SAUCE

1 cup fresh raspberries

¹/₄ cup sugar

FORCE RASPBERRIES THROUGH A SIEVE FINE ENOUGH TO HOLD BACK THE SEEDS. PLACE INTO A SAUCEPAN, ADD SUGAR AND COOK OVER MODERATE HEAT FOR 10 MINUTES, OR LONG ENOUGH TO MAKE A HEAVY SYRUP. SERVE COLD.

-Antoine's, New Orleans, Louisiana

PEACH MELBA SUNDAE

Dip 3 large scoops of vanilla ice cream into a tall sundae goblet and cover with Melba sauce. Add fresh sliced peaches, garnish with whipped cream, and place a maraschino cherry at the top.

-Jaxson's Ice Cream Parlor, Dania, Florida

Chapter 9

THE DECADE THAT ROARED

"It was an age of miracles, it was an age of art, it was an age of excess, it was an age of satire."

—F. SCOTT FITZGERALD

How ya gonna wet your whistle when the whole darn world goes dry? By the end of winter in 1920, legal alcohol was already a fond and fading memory. During the following 12 years, 10 months and 19 days, the country experienced an era of corruption, scandal, gangsters, smuggling, jazz, tabloids, wealth, flagpole-sitting, bobbed hair and a dizzying whirl of ice cream. Good heavens, what a time it was!

Prohibition forced the conversion of many town taverns into soda fountains. Adolph Coors converted his brewery to a malted milk plant before throwing himself off a hotel balcony. At Anheuser-Busch, the St. Louis brewery, gallons of ice cream rolled out of the cold rooms instead of barreled beer.

SENSE OF HUMOR

In 1920, Harry Burt, an ice cream parlor operator in Youngstown, Ohio, put an ice cream bar on a stick (copying the lollypop), and sold his new invention from a white truck, outfitted with bells to attract kids of all ages. His "Good Humor Man" wore the pressed and spotless white uniform of a soda jerk, with white hat, shiny Sam Browne belt and black bow tie. He was always very courteous, raising his cap to women and providing men with a crisp salute.

Commercial production of ice cream gathered steam and swelled to an incredible 150 million gallons during the first tumultuous year of Prohibition. The addition of extra milk solids, with higher butterfat content and more sugar, turned out smoother, richer ice cream, just as those surprising concoctions called sundaes came of age.

History itself seemed to accelerate to double-time, and the lightning tempo of the decade produced an abundance of new amusements. Teenagers watched double features, ate double dip cones and shared double scoop sundaes. Everybody, it seemed, wanted twice as much of everything good. The Twin Sundae, which tumbled out of a Midwestern drugstore, was a doubly delectable dessert with two scoops of ice cream, one beside the other, with toppings of choice.

The speakeasy was the destination of choice for some couples. For others, the next best thing to legal booze was homemade: industrial alcohol, juniper berries and glycerin mixed in bathtubs, dangerous and just barely palatable. When it was discovered that the sweetness of chocolate killed the exceedingly bitter taste of synthetic gin, candy bars joined silver flasks in pockets and purses.

Indulgence boomed, including indulgence in both ice cream treats and other sweets. Nickel candies, including Mounds, Milky Way, Reese's Peanut Butter Cup and Tootsie Roll, were all launched during Prohibition, and candy toppings began turning up on ice cream sundaes.

By 1929, sixty percent of the country's 58,258 drugstores had installed soda fountains. They were the most popular public gathering places in a dry America, leading one British visitor to observe that "young people do not go for country walks in America. They chiefly consort in the ice cream parlor."

THE RECIPES

ONE FREE HOUR
IN THE CANDY STORE

Dip 3 large scoops of vanilla ice cream into a tall sundae goblet and cover with hot fudge. Top with Reese's Pieces and M &Ms, garnish with whipped cream, and place a maraschino cherry at the top.

  --Eveready Diner, Hyde Park, New York

SNICKER DOODLE SUNDAE

Dip 2 large scoops of vanilla ice cream into a tall sundae goblet and cover with chocolate syrup. Top with pieces of a chopped Snickers candy bar, garnish with whipped cream and place a maraschino cherry at the top.

  -Beaver Island Lodge, Beaver Island, Michigan

SUNDAE SHOPPING

During the 1920s, Woolworth's began installing soda fountains in its five-and-ten-cent stores. When you placed your order for a sundae, the lady behind the counter, dressed in a starched pink uniform, would serve it to you in a tulip-shaped glass. Those magical fountains encouraged people to treat the store as a general gathering place, much like a food court in today's shopping malls.

Chapter 10

ELECTRIC SUNDAE

> *"In real life, unlike in Shakespeare, the sweetness of the rose depends upon the name it bears."*
>
> —HUBERT H. HUMPHREY

Many sundaes have "humorous titles," which is how William S. Adkins described the odd names of some ice cream concoctions in a 1933 issue of *Druggists Circular*. Adkins suggested a dish called the "Electric Sundae", which he said could be "advertised as having plenty of juice and currants." He went on to explain how to make it and who would appreciate it: "Fruit syrup is poured over ice cream and sprinkled with currants. A novelty of this nature goes well at a college grill, young blades deriving infinite entertainment through explaining the proposition to each newcomer."

The Dispenser's Formulary, a sort of soda jerk's bible first published in 1896, eventually had recipes for no fewer than 562 sundaes, each with a fanciful name, such as Hot Temptation or Cupid's Delight.

Some sundaes were named after important events. Following several unsuccessful attempts to reach the North Pole, the American explorer Robert E. Peary sailed north on the 184-ton *Roosevelt* for another try. Peary drove a dogsled four hundred miles from his ship and stood at the North Pole on April 6, 1909. The cold was so intense, as he told it, that a flask of brandy carried under his parka froze solid. In an edition published six years later, *The Dispenser's Formulary* described not one, but two sundaes, commemorating Peary's Arctic conquest.

"ROOSEVELT" SPECIAL

At one end of a banana boat place a large scoop of strawberry ice cream, and at the other, a large scoop of vanilla ice cream (strawberry represents the ship, vanilla represents an iceberg). Cover the vanilla with crushed pineapple, and the strawberry with red raspberries and chopped mixed nuts. Place two Nabisco wafers on the edge, one on either side of the strawberry ice cream, and pointing toward the vanilla. Then, put two Nabiscos in a vertical position on top of the strawberry to represent sails.

NORTH POLE SUNDAE

Split one large banana lengthwise, and arrange on a long plate to represent the runners of a sleigh. On these and to represent a "pack", add one large scoop of vanilla ice cream, and to simulate the snow effect, cover the "pack" with marshmallow syrup. On one end of the plate put a small candy polar bear; at the other end, put six small jelly gum drops. On top of the ice cream place a small American flag.

Sundae naming remained something of an American mania in the decades before World War II. Fixing names to particular sundae recipes both established their identities and created the expectation of uniformity.

The best sundaes are quick works of simple art, logically and carefully composed, with the best ingredients. First comes the visual satisfaction, then the name. The final test is the taste. A great name can't raise a sundae with inferior ingredients to stardom but, assuming the best components, a clever name makes a sundae stick in a customer's memory.

Practically impossible to forget is a showy sundae served at Green Mill restaurants, a Minnesota-based chain of casual eateries. "The Inside-Out Sundae was the brainstorm of a guy from our Duluth store," says Todd King, president of the company. "It's not only a name customers remember, it truly describes the concept."

King is a scrappy, competitive guy whose background includes running a Dairy Queen franchise. But the Inside-Out Sundae is definitely not a fast-food candidate. It requires time-consuming preparation. "We sometimes 'punish' crybabies who show up late for work by putting them on the sundae detail," admits King.

After a coating of hot fudge and caramel is slathered on the *outside* of sundae goblets, they are held in a freezer awaiting customers' orders. When ready to serve, the goblets are filled with vanilla ice cream and strawberries, and topped with whipped cream and chopped nuts.

And what's the proper technique for eating one? According to King, the same way you would usually eat a sundae—on the inside. Just don't forget to scrape off the good stuff on the outside.

IN NAME ONLY

The sundae's good name has been borrowed for a few goofy-sounding but good-tasting dishes that have nothing to do with ice cream. The Turkey Sundae, as conceived at the Cadillac Café in Los Angeles, is constructed with roasted turkey slices leaning against a tower of mashed potatoes. It's topped with gravy and crowned with cranberry sauce and sliced almonds. In Christiansburg, Virginia, Beamer's Restaurant (owned by Frank Beamer, head football coach of the Virginia Tech Hokies) serves a Meatloaf Sundae, mounded high with mashed potatoes and topped with gravy and fried onions. But nothing is quite like the Chili Sundae at Tony Packo's in Toledo, Ohio. Just imagine a tall sundae goblet filled with hot chili and sour cream in place of vanilla ice cream and syrup, shaved cheese as the alternative to whipped cream, and a cherry tomato on top instead of you-know-what.

THE RECIPES

INSIDE-OUT SUNDAE

4 ounces hot fudge

4 ounces caramel

¹/₄ cup honey-roasted peanuts

1 scoop vanilla ice cream

4 ounces strawberry topping

1. PAINT HOT FUDGE ON HALF OF THE EXTERIOR OF A TULIP GLASS AND CARAMEL ON THE OTHER HALF.

2. SPRINKLE CHOPPED PEANUTS ON THE HOT FUDGE AND CARAMEL.

3. FREEZE THE GLASS FOR UP TO AN HOUR.

4. SCOOP VANILLA ICE CREAM INTO PRE-COATED GLASS.

5. Cover ice cream with strawberries and top with whipped cream and a cherry.

6. Top contents of the glass with hot fudge.

7. Drizzle medium-size round plate with hot fudge and place the sundae glass in the center of plate.

8. Sprinkle plate with chopped peanuts.

-The Green Mill, St. Paul, Minnesota

HOT FUDGE BAGEL SUPREME

This odd coupling perches a hot fudge sundae atop a bagel that has been soaked in crème de cacao.

1 cinnamon-raisin bagel, sliced

2 teaspoons dark crème de cacao

1 scoop vanilla ice cream

4 ounces hot fudge sauce

3 tablespoons chopped walnuts

Dab of whipped cream

2 maraschino cherries

Toast bagel and prick both halves with a fork. In a shallow dish, soak bagel halves in crème de cacao for 15 minutes. Put 1 bagel half, sliced side up, in a dessert dish. Top with ice cream, then second bagel half, sliced side down. Heat fudge topping. Pour over bagel. Top with nuts, garnish with whipped cream, and place maraschino cherries at the top.

-from *Bagelmania* by Connie Berman and Suzanne Munshower

Chapter 11

CALIFORNIA DREAMERS

"Originality is simply a pair of fresh eyes."

—THOMAS WENTWORTH HIGGINSON

*I*n the beginning, the sundae was made with vanilla, chocolate or straw-berry ice cream. For the first 30 or so years of its life, that was that. But the sameness was shattered a few weeks after the October stock market crash of 1929. Something was added to ice cream on its way to hard times.

Only a year before, two gentlemen by the name of William Dreyer and Joseph Edy shook hands and agreed to become partners in a small ice cream factory at 3315 Grand Avenue in Oakland, California, and the Grand Ice Cream Company was born. German-born Dreyer, who had experience as an ice cream maker, had opened an ice creamery in Visalia, deep in California dairy country. Joseph Edy had learned candy making at the side of his mother in Montana before he moved south to open a candy shop in Oakland. Their combined skills got their new company off to a good start.

Dreyer was recruited to Oakland to run the National Ice Cream plant, but a better opportunity presented itself in the person of Edy. By 1928, they had established an estimable partnership, one that combined Dreyer's ice cream expertise and Edy's candy-making skills.

The Great Depression presented a rough, rocky road for entrepreneurs and practically everybody else. Dreyer and Edy had the notion of making an original chocolate ice cream by adding to it roasted nuts and marsh-mallows, typical sundae toppings. They experimented with walnuts, but wal-nuts gave the ice cream a bitter taste, and the nuts became a bit soggy. So the partners tried mixing in lightly-roasted almonds. The nuts stayed crisp; the chocolate ice cream remained sweet. The fellows liked their new ice cream and thought the public would, too. So they decided to go ahead even though making batches of the stuff was an exacting task. Edy used his wife's sewing shears, regularly dipped into hot water, to cut standard marshmallows into bite-size pieces.

A Dreyer's driver cranks up a delivery truck in a circa 1930 photo.

"Dreyer and Edy named their creation Rocky Road, not only because it described the mouth-feel of the flavor they had created, but because they believed it was a comment on the times," says John Harrison, Dreyer's Grand Ice Cream's "Official Taster" and flavor developer. "They did something no one had ever done before. They put a sundae *inside* the ice cream."

It's a measure of the high esteem with which Dreyer's holds him that Harrison alone is allowed to monitor the quality standards of its ice creams. Like Clark Kent, who ducks into a phone booth to slip into his Superman duds, the mild-mannered Harrison puts on his white laboratory coat and black bowtie early each morning to prepare for the day's challenges.

Actually, his lifestyle is molded by the sacrifices a bold taster must make. Harrison avoids eating spicy foods or wearing aftershave, lest a strong taste or fragrance compromise the perfect neutrality of his taste buds. He is determined to save mankind, one lick at a time, from inferior ice creams.

He tastes vanilla first to clear the palate before fastidiously working his way to chocolate chip cookie dough or mint chocolate chip or any flavor of more textural complexity. With a gold spoon clasped firmly in hand, he scoops a small amount off the top of a half-gallon carton to test for taste, then digs deeper to test for body and texture. "First, I put a sample on my tongue," explains Harrison. "Then I aerate it by smacking my lips and bringing in the ambient room temperature, warming it up some more and driving that top bouquet up to the olfactory nerves. After I roll it around for four or five seconds, I spit it into a 55-gallon trash barrel."

Like a wine judge, Harrison doesn't swallow the ice cream. He finishes his tasting by late morning to avoid palate fatigue.

In 1983, he was eating a scoop of vanilla along with a plate of cookies in the company's ice cream parlor when he thought to himself, "Why not save a step and put a cookie in the ice cream?" He experimented with 15 different commercial brands of cookie before he determined that Oreos matched best with the ice cream. It was a marriage made in Oakland. The Dreyer's marketing team came up with the name, Cookies 'N' Cream, and now it's the fifth best-selling flavor in the United States, under the Dreyer's name in 14 Western states and under the Edy's label east of the Mississippi.

"The matrix of a real sundae is the best possible vanilla ice cream," declares Harrison. "It ought to have the appearance of cream, not stark white, not bright yellow. As for flavor, the balance of dairy note, sugar and added ingredients is critical. And the body must be clean and free of coarseness or icy crystals, the texture chewy but not gummy." He confesses that his three favorite flavors are Vanilla, Vanilla Bean and French Vanilla.

GOING FOR THE GOLD

Ghirardelli Chocolate Company's history dates back to California's gold rush, when Domingo Ghirardelli, an Italian confectioner, began importing cocoa beans and other essential commodities from South America to supply the needs of the mining communities. He eventually opened a chocolate factory facing North Point Street in San Francisco's waterfront district.

Today, the flagship Ghirardelli soda fountain whips up a world-class hot fudge "Bonanza" sundae, which can be made with Turkish Coffee Ice Cream if you so choose. "The Rock," a chocolate-armored vanilla island in a whipped-cream bay, is as formidable as Alcatraz before it became a tourist site. Rivers of chocolate syrup running over three marshmallow-covered chocolate ice cream scoops, studded with nuts and chocolate nuggets, mark a sundae well named "Strike It Rich."

GOOD AS FATHER USED TO MAKE

In 1948, a California dreamer by the name of Earle Swensen opened a dipping parlor in San Francisco atop Russian Hill, promoting his ice cream as "Good as Father Used to Make." He eventually sold the Swensen name to franchise managers who've opened more than 300 shops worldwide, but the original Swensen's look hasn't changed much, and it still serves some of the best sundaes in the West.

IRISH COFFEE MACAROONEY

Dip 2 large scoops of coffee ice cream into a tall sundae goblet. Smother with crushed macaroons, garnish with whipped cream and place a maraschino cherry at the top.

GOLD RUSH

Dip one large scoop of chocolate ice cream into a sundae goblet and cover with hot fudge sauce. Add one large scoop of coffee ice cream and cover with hot butterscotch sauce. Garnish with a sprinkle of sliced almonds and whipped cream. Top with a maraschino.

—Swenson's, San Francisco, California

FORCING
PUSHING
JAMMING
DOWN
That First Scoop
of Ice Cream
Into
the SUNDAE Glass
Means
OVER PORTIONS
and
LOSS

DEPRESSION ERA INSTRUCTIONS FOR SODA JERKS

THE RECIPES

BLACK AND TAN SUNDAE

Not all sundaes are inside the ice cream at Dreyer's. The company has long operated the Ice Cream Shoppe, which serves many traditional sundaes at its original College Avenue location, in the same building that serves as corporate headquarters.

• •

DIP ONE LARGE SCOOP OF VANILLA ICE CREAM AND ONE LARGE SCOOP OF ROCKY ROAD ICE CREAM SIDE-BY-SIDE INTO A WIDE SUNDAE BOWL. COVER THE VANILLA WITH CHOCOLATE SAUCE AND THE ROCKY ROAD WITH CARAMEL SAUCE. GARNISH WITH WHIPPED CREAM, SPRINKLE WITH CHOPPED MIXED NUTS AND PLACE A CHERRY AT THE TOP.

• •

—Dreyer's Ice Cream Shoppe, Oakland, California

Chapter 12

SUNDAE BIBLE

*"We got the hot fudge on the bottom . . . that allows
you to control the fudge distribution while you're
eating your ice cream.."*

—JERRY SEINFELD

he prospects of the cigar dimmed as Americans made the switch to
smoking cigarettes. By the time Howard Dearing Johnson inherited his father's wholesale cigar business, it was heavily in debt, so he
had little alternative but to liquidate the remaining inventory and close up
shop. When the smoke cleared, he'd sold his yellow Stutz Bearcat and put
it toward the purchase of a small corner drug store in his hometown of
Wollaston, Massachusetts. It was 1925, and Howard Johnson—called
Buster by his family—was 28, scrappy and determined.

While his store offered candy, newspapers and apothecary accessories,

A PRISTINE HO JO FOUNTAIN BEFORE THE OPENING BELL.

THE INSIDE SCOOP

In 1930, Sherman Kelly of Toledo, Ohio, set out to improve the ice cream scoop. The result was the Zeroll—a non-mechanical, one-handed scoop—which was a time-saver for soda jerks who struggled with rock-hard ice cream. Its thick handle is comfortable for large and small hands, and its self-defrosting liquid (which responds to heat from the user's hand) contributes to perfect release, leaving only traces of melted cream inside the scoop. The beauty and utility of the Zeroll design has been recognized by and displayed at the Museum of Modern Art in New York City.

Johnson found that the real money was to be made at his marble-top soda fountain. He reckoned that if ice cream was so popular, then better-tasting ice cream would be even more popular.

Howard Johnson came up with what he often referred to as his "secret formula" for vanilla and chocolate ice creams. The poorly-kept secret was, in fact, all natural ingredients and twice the normal content of butterfat. Soon there were long lines of customers waiting outside as his workers hand-cranked ice cream inside.

When warm weather arrived, Johnson opened a beachfront ice cream stand, and during that first summer sold $60,000 worth of ice cream cones—at a nickel a cone. The good old days are when you make them, and by 1928, Johnson's cash registers rang up ice cream sales to the tune of $240,000. He kept thinking up new flavors until he reached 28 varieties. "I thought I had every flavor in the world," he remembered. "The 28 flavors became my trademark."

His success could hardly be ignored, and he was able to convince some otherwise skeptical bankers to lend him enough money to open a restaurant in nearby Quincy. It occupied the main floor of the town's first sky-scraper, a ten-story granite building that just happened to be owned by the bank. The first Howard Johnson's restaurant featured fried clams, baked beans, chicken pies, frankfurters and ten-cent ice cream sundaes.

Home of the original father-and-son presidents, John and John Quincy

BASIC TRAINING

This is the mandated procedure for scooping ice cream from Howard Johnson's Fountain Service Manual.

A. Shake scoop to remove excess water.

B. Hold the scoop firmly, with your thumb under the release. The closer your hand is to the head of the scoop, the better leverage you have. This lessens the strain on your wrist.

C. With the scoop <u>facing</u> <u>you</u>, dip into the ice cream approximately $1/4$ inch. <u>Do</u> <u>not</u> face the scoop downward

D. Draw the scoop toward you, along the edge of the container, in a clockwise motion. The ice cream is forced into one side of the scoop and out the opposite side, forming a "lip."

E. When the portions have been removed, the container should appear with the ice cream higher in the middle than at the side.

Adams, the town of Quincy has always cherished its Yankee heritage. So when it came time to decorate the restaurant, Johnson faced it with colonial-style white clapboard and placed homey, glowing lamps in fake dormer windows. The knotty pine paneling and ruffled curtains filled out a design one architectural historian has called "a beacon of traditional values."

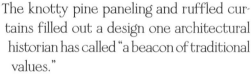

It was the heart of the Depression and there was little money available to borrow for further expansion, so Johnson embarked on a daring experiment, one that would have great impact on the course of American business. In 1935, he persuaded former schoolmate Reginald Sprague to open his own "Howard Johnson's" restaurant in Orleans on Cape Cod as part of a franchise agreement.

Johnson was a stickler for details.

He insisted that the restaurant be run according to strict guidelines and use precise food preparation procedures, or the contract would be voided and Sprague would have to remove the Howard Johnson sign. It was Johnson's way or the highway.

Home-style food was served by waitresses in prim, starched blue and orange dresses. Sprague and subsequent franchisees adhered to what they called the "Howard Johnson Bible," a written set of standards for cleanliness, service, menu items and recipes, devised by the tireless Howard

FAMILY FRIENDLY

On July 18, 1935, in Springfield, Massachusetts, two young brothers, 20-year-old Prestley Blake and 18-year-old Curtis Blake, borrowed $300 to open a modest neighborhood sweet shop called "Friendly Ice Cream," selling double-dip cones for five cents—just two cents more than a first-class stamp. In 1979, the two brothers sold what had become a chain of Friendly's restaurants for $162 million. Today, Friendly's restaurants have replaced many Howard Johnson's locations in the northeast.

HEATH BAR TOFFEE CRUNCH SUNDAE

Dip 2 large scoops of vanilla ice cream into a large sundae goblet. Ladle on 2 ounces each of caramel syrup, hot fudge, and marshmallow crème. Garnish with whipped cream and sprinkle crushed Heath Bars over top.

MARVELOUS & MAGNIFICENT SUNDAE

Dip 2 large scoops of vanilla ice cream into a large sundae goblet. Ladle on 2 ounces each of hot fudge and marshmallow crème. Garnish with whipped cream and sprinkle M&Ms (plain or peanut) over top.

–Friendly's Ice Cream Restaurants, 530 locations in 16 states

Johnson. He would allow no variation from one unit to the next, as Howard Johnson's restaurants sprung up from Maine to Florida.

Ice cream sundaes were topped not only with whipped cream, nuts and a cherry, but also an oval shaped sugar cookie embossed with the Howard Johnson's logo. The fine points of sundae-making included a #16 conical scoop and adherence to a step-by-step procedure.

As America became a nation in a hurry, Howard Johnson's eventually lost out to fast food competitors. At its peak in the 1970s, the chain could boast nearly 1,000 locations, but today you have to look long and hard to find the few that remain. Some say the Ho Jo's in New York's Times Square should have lasted forever, but after 46 years, on July 9, 2005, the restaurant served its last sundae and closed.

Chapter 13

VICTORY SUNDAES

"The destiny of nations depends on the manner in which they nourish themselves."

—JEAN ANTHELME BRILLAT-SAVARIN

You just called it "The War." Everyone knew exactly what you were talking about. Americans waved tearful goodbyes to their loved ones in uniform as they set out for duty in Europe or the South Pacific. A late 1941 editorial in the New Republic made the case emphatically: "The dirt farmer in the corn belt, the salesgirl behind the counter, the miner at the coal field, the stoker at sea—all believe in our democracy and demand vigorously that it be defended."

Culture is not only what we live by. It is also, in large measure, what we live for.

We remember best those things that lie close to the heart, things we cherish. In setting out on this enterprise, the American soldier needed a symbol for everything that was homebred, homemade and good about "back home." Simple and innocent, ice cream stirred joyous recollections of the malt shop, and memories of the girlfriend who was waiting there. Decades later, Sarah Schulman wrote, "Ice cream . . . a food that tastes so good in the mouth it makes a person feel human again. It brings back memories. It reminds a guy of other things."

Ice cream sundaes and the local soda fountain stood for something in those days, as everyone pulled together against those who mocked our sweet indulgence. One newspaper report quoted a German officer's comment: "We do not fear a nation of ice cream eaters."

The Army Quartermaster Corps regularly shipped dehydrated ice cream mix to U.S. army bases around the world. Many soldiers carried rations of the powder, and once they followed instructions for making something resembling ice cream, they could turn it into sundaes by covering the so-called ice cream with canned fruit, crushed candy or any sweet topping they could put their hands on.

Of all the odd things that happened during the war, surely the sweetest oddity was a report of airmen on bombing missions who simultaneously made ice cream. It seems some crews placed a can of the cream mixture in the rear compartment of a B-29, and by the time they returned from a sortie, freezing high-altitude temperatures and the plane's vibration had combined to produce a batch of ice cream, ready to eat.

Meanwhile, Secretary of the Navy James Forrestal commissioned the war's most unusual ship at a cost of a million dollars. It was the Navy's "Ice Cream Barge," the world's first floating ice cream parlor. Its sole responsibility was to produce ice cream for sailors in the Pacific theater. The plant turned out 1,500 gallons of edible morale every hour.

On the home front, the Ice Cream Merchandising Institute, a pro-

AN ADVERTISEMENT PUBLISHED IN THE SODA FOUNTAIN AND QUICK FOOD-SERVICE *MAGAZINE, AUGUST, 1942.*

motional arm of the dairy industry, created a World War II "Victory Sundae" campaign. Participating merchants included a Defense Savings Stamp with every ice cream sundae sold; including the specially concocted All-American Sundae. Their slogan was "Keep 'Em Buying to Keep 'Em Flying."

YANKEE INGENUITY

During the war, sailor Butch Baskin was stationed in the South Seas, assigned to supply detail. In a strategic deal, Baskin bartered the company jeep for an ice cream freezer from a visiting aircraft carrier. He doctored up bland military-issue ice cream mixture with native tropical fruits and exotic nuts, and his wartime flavors became the stuff of legend.

At the war's end Baskin partnered with his brother-in-law, Irv Robbins, perfecting recipes for the flavors he had made in his commandeered ice cream freezer. The ambitious young men were operating six ice cream stores in the Los Angeles area when they dreamed up the "31" concept—an ice cream flavor for each day of the month, and three more than offered at Howard Johnson's. At each Baskin-Robbins café, old school desks served as tables, and soda jerks provided miniature pink spoons for sampling. Americans flocked to Baskin-Robbins to have their favorite fresh-fruit flavors served in "healthy" portions. By 1959, there were 500 franchised locations, all decorated in bold, bright colors. Time Magazine described them as "polka-dotted pleasure palaces."

Food writer Gael Greene declared, "If I have only one life to live, let me live next door to Baskin-Robbins and its incredible changing parade of 31 flavors."

THE RECIPES

MACARTHUR BLITZ SUNDAE

In 1942, with so many young Americans in the thick of the conflict, this formula appeared in the trade magazine, Soda Fountain.

1 chocolate bomb (large scoop of chocolate)	Shot with chocolate sauce (1 1/2 ounces)
1 vanilla grenade (large scoop of vanilla)	Sprayed with salted peanuts (2 teaspoons of Spanish peanuts)

USE A TULIP SUNDAE GLASS. PLACE CHOCOLATE ICE CREAM ON BOTTOM, THEN VANILLA ICE CREAM ON TOP. CHOCOLATE SAUCE COVERS THE VANILLA. COVER ALL WITH SPANISH PEANUTS. NO OTHER TRIMMING NECESSARY.

YANKEE DOODLE DANDY

In its seventh decade, this sundae is still a winner on the Fourth of July. Three cheers for the red, white and blue!

1/4 cup marshmallow syrup	2 tablespoons crushed maraschino cherries
2 large scoops vanilla ice cream	2 tablespoons blueberries

POUR HALF OF THE MARSHMALLOW SYRUP INTO THE BOTTOM OF A WIDE SUNDAE GLASS AND ADD THE ICE CREAM. TOP WITH THE REMAINDER OF THE MARSHMALLOW SYRUP AND PLACE THE CHERRIES ON ONE SIDE OF THE GLASS AND THE BLUEBERRIES ON THE OPPOSITE SIDE, LEAVING A WHITE STRIPE DOWN THE MIDDLE.

Chapter 14

SODA FOUNTAIN CODE

You scream, I scream,
They all scream for ice cream.
Tuesdays, Mondays,
They all scream for Sundaes.
—COLLEGE CHEER, 1920S

"Drop a bucket of mud with a black bottom!" Translation: Dish up a hot fudge sundae with chocolate ice cream.

What you just heard was a waiter barking an order to a soda jerk at the old Jayhawk Café in the college town of Lawrence, Kansas, but something like it would have been said at practically any ice cream fountain during the glory days of the '20s and '30s.

Paul Sinclair started his own career as a waiter at this finishing school for soda jerks. Eventually, he purchased it. Shoptalk at the Jayhawk provided some colorful entertainment, but, more important, it shortened the time it took to place orders.

Soda fountain vernacular or "calls" varied from region to region and applied to more than ice cream concoctions. If you heard "Adam and Eve on a raft," it probably meant poached eggs on toast. For scrambled eggs with an English muffin, the order was "wreck 'em and burn the British."

"Life preservers" were doughnuts, and "sweep the kitchen" was a plate of hash.

Ice cream dishes, of course, were soda fountain staples. If you heard the yell, "twist it, choke it, make it cackle," someone had ordered a chocolate malted egg cream.

"Drop" was a single scoop, "burn a snowball" for chocolate ice cream, and "throw in the mud" added hot fudge. For a second scoop of ice cream, you might have heard "put a hat on it." A call of "Chicago" requested a pineapple sundae. "Shake one in the hay," a strawberry milkshake. The banana split was known in some quarters as a "farmer's lunch." Ice cream dishes were served with "Adam's ale" (glass of water) or "balloon juice" (seltzer), and whenever something ran out, it was "86ed."

Calls also provided coded exchanges among members of the staff for things other than food. A call of "ninety-five" sounded the alarm when a customer was skipping out on the bill. "Ninety-nine" referred to the head soda jerk, and "ninety-eight" to the assistant. "Eighty-seven and a half," announced

COUNTER INTELLIGENCE

The centerpiece of the soda fountain was a tap from which mineral water (the first soda) was drawn. The moniker "soda jerk" came from the jerking motions required to spray foamy carbonation into syrups from the pumps and levers behind the counter.

The soda jerk was also known as the "fizzician," an expert at adding fizz to a soda or syrup to a sundae. A good fizzician also knew exactly how much topping to ladle on: if too little was added, the syrup would be gone before the ice cream; too much and a puddle remained after the ice cream was gone. A well-trained soda jerk never let syrups run over the edge of the sundae glass and never ever gave out spoons with sticky handles.

An appropriate cracker accompanied each sundae. With chocolate, coffee, and maple, a salty cracker was acceptable; with fruit or fruit flavors, a sweet cracker was more correct. And, without waiting for a customer request, a glass of iced water was dutifully served with each and every sundae.

The white caps worn by soda jerks in American pharmacies and ice cream parlors in the 1930s and 1940s were inspired by military apparel. Some say druggists and other owners of soda fountains adopted them to lend authority to fountain workers.

THE SODA FOUNTAIN *BY WILLIAM GLACKENS, 1935.*

there was a looker out front, and screwballs behind the counter called "fix the pumps" when directing attention to a coed in a tight sweater.

In 1941, *Drug Store Management*, a magazine for the trade, scolded fountain operators for permitting the use of slang in their establishments, pointing out that "it tends to reduce the formality of the occasion and may perhaps suggest a lack of respect for the customer's order."

GRACE UNDER PRESSURE

During high school, Charles Goetz worked part-time as a soda jerk at an ice cream parlor near the University of Illinois when whipped cream topping for ice cream sundaes had to be beaten by hand. In 1931, as a senior chemistry major, he experimented with pressurizing cream with gas and releasing it as a foam. The gas he used was the odorless, tasteless, non-flammable nitrous oxide used as an anesthetic by dentists. Goetz had produced the world's first commercial whipped cream from a can.

THE RECIPE

HOT FUDGE WAFFLE DISH SUNDAE

The Jayhawk Café is gone, but today's students at the University of Kansas still love their ice cream. "Sundae Socials" mark campus social life (as they do at several other colleges), and downtown Lawrence boasts an ice cream parlor across from the old Varsity Theater, which serves sundaes in waffles, made in an old-fashioned waffle iron and then molded in a bowl shape over an old malt cup. The parlor is called Sylas and Maddy's, signifying not a new direction in ice cream talk, but the names of its owners' pets, a red tabby (Sylas) and a terrier mix (Maddy).

DIP 2 LARGE SCOOPS OF VANILLA BEAN ICE CREAM INTO A WAFFLE DISH. CUT ONE BANANA INTO SLICES AND PLACE AROUND THE ICE CREAM, THEN LADLE 2 OUNCES OF HOT FUDGE SAUCE TO COVER. GARNISH WITH WHIPPED CREAM, SPRINKLE ON SLICED TOASTED ALMONDS, AND PLACE A MARASCHINO CHERRY AT THE TOP.

-Sylas and Maddy's, Lawrence, Kansas

Chapter 15

SODA JERK HALL OF FAME

"Don't I look like a film director?"

—JOHN LLOYD SULLIVAN (JOEL MCCREA)

"No, you look more like a soda jerk."

— HOBO

—FROM SULLIVAN'S TRAVELS BY PRESTON STURGES

*I*n 1938, there was a revolt of sorts when the soda fountain staff at the University of Michigan decided they no longer wanted to be dubbed "jerks." They must have had it up to here with the kidding. Local protesters organized the "Society for the Prevention of Cruelty to Soda Jerkers Who Want to be Known as Fountaineers of America." Thankfully, the long-winded term never caught on.

Over the years, soda jerks have included some of our greatest comedians, actors, writers, musicians and politicians.

It wasn't long after the girls voted Bob Dole the best-looking boy in high school that he got a job as soda jerk at Dawson's Drug on Main Street in his hometown of Russell, Kansas. It was there that he learned "the flip"—the art of tossing a scoop of ice cream into the air then catching it in a dish—before putting the finishing touches on a sundae. And he liked eating his own creations. "In my first two weeks on the job I put on nine pounds," remembers the former U.S. senator.

The fifth of seven children, Leslie Townes Hope was a teenage soda jerk in Cleveland, Ohio. Too bad there's no record of the jokes he cracked at the fountain because he grew up to be comedian Bob Hope.

Another Ohio talent ushered at the Walnut Hills Orpheus in Cincinnati and worked as a soda jerk in a drugstore near the movie house. This ambitious young man later made it big in Hollywood as Tyrone Power.

The Depression was hard on his family, so Gene Kelly worked two jobs during the summers to put himself through Penn State. He drove a truck for a construction company at 25 cents an hour, eight hours a day, six days a week. At night he worked as a soda jerk for Reymer's Candy Company, then home of what some said were the best ice cream sundaes in Pittsburgh. "I arrived in Hollywood twenty pounds overweight and as strong as an ox," he later confessed, "so when I put on a white tie and tails like Astaire, I still looked like a truck driver."

"Mr. Halston," the designer who dressed some very stylish women, was Roy Halston from Evansville, Indiana, who worked as a soda jerk at the Merry-Go-Round Drive-In before he came to New York.

Malcolm Little was a soda jerk at the Townsend Drug Store in the Boston neighborhood of Roxbury. He would become fiery African-American preacher and revolutionary, Malcolm X.

In his autobiography, *David Brinkley: A Memoir*, the distinguished newscaster recalled his youth at Wrightsville Beach, North Carolina. He wrote, "For a schoolboy with a summer job at the beach making a little money working as a soda jerk . . . with girls all around in swimsuits that then seemed skimpy, the beach, the surf—it was heaven."

Like many important figures in history, Harry Truman was an energetic

COURTESY OF JACKSON COUNTY [MO] HISTORICAL SOCIETY.

THE CLINTON DRUG STORE, AS IT LOOKED WHEN HARRY TRUMAN JERKED THERE.

man with an enormous capacity for hard work. He spent his youth and young adulthood in Independence, Missouri, a town not far from Kansas City. Mornings, from seven o'clock until school time, he mopped the floor, cleaned away the trash and polished the prescription bottles at Jim Clinton's Drugstore. On weekends he made ice cream, jerked at the soda fountain and waited on customers. Young Harry's salary was $3 a week. "It was a great day all around when I got that $3," former President Truman recalled in his later years.

Clinton's, on West Maple Street, hums along today under the auspices of the local historical society. Its business has been distilled to a soda foun-

THOSE TWO JERKS

In the 1948 film <u>Who Done It</u>, *Chick (Bud Abbott) and Mervin (Lou Costello) are working as soda jerks.*

"I ordered an ice cream sundae," barks Chick.

Mervin replies, "You did? What day is it today?"

A STAR IS BORN

In 1923, Russian-born immigrant Samuel Born established the Just Born Candy Company, a small candy-making factory and retail shop in Brooklyn, New York. That's where he invented those tiny chocolate things you sprinkle over a sundae. An employee named James Bartholomew operated the machine making the new candy, so Born christened the confection in his honor. He called them "jimmies," a term still used in the northeast. In other parts of the country they are known as sparkles, toppettes, trimettes, shots or candy ants.

tain, and the store does a bang-up business at the six counter stools and eight tables under walls lined with photographs of its past and other memorabilia. Visitors order from a nostalgic menu of phosphates, shakes and malteds, ice cream sodas and dishes, including the late President's favorite: a chocolate ice cream sundae.

THE RECIPES

HARRY TRUMAN SUNDAE

Dip one large scoop of chocolate ice cream into a sundae tulip. Cover the ice cream with butterscotch syrup, garnish with whipped cream and place a maraschino cherry at the top.

-Clinton's Drugstore, Independence, Missouri

GEORGE BAILEY SUNDAE

Remember Mr. Gower's drugstore and soda fountain in Frank Capra's holiday classic? In It's a Wonderful Life, young George Bailey labors as a soda jerk, while a flirtatious eight-year-old Violet Bick orders candy and angles for George's attention. Also sitting at the counter is young Mary Hatch, the childhood sweetheart he will eventually marry. Mary orders a chocolate sundae, but rejects George's offer of coconut on top. George tells Mary that coconuts come from Tahiti, the Fiji Islands and the Coral Sea, and boasts that he plans to visit all of those places.

DIP 2 SCOOPS OF COCONUT ALMOND JOY ICE CREAM INTO A LARGE SUNDAE GOBLET. COVER WITH HOT FUDGE AND SPRINKLE WITH SHREDDED COCONUT.

-*Dr. Jazz Soda Fountain* & Grille, Lebanon, Illinois

Chapter 16

SUNDAE DRIVE

"Whither goest thou, America, in thy shiny car?"

—JACK KEROUAC

By the late 1940s and through the '50s, happy days were here again. The country was bustling; veterans and their families were flocking to new suburbs, financing home ownership with the help of the G.I. bill, and buying cars just as fast as Detroit could build them. "See the U.S.A. in your Chevrolet" was one advertising slogan that put Americans on wheels.

Sundaes belonged to the weekend. In *Familiar Territory*, Joseph Epstein observes, "the Sunday drive usually had no greater goal than a longish ride for an ice cream soda or sundae."

Thomas Andreas Carvelas had Americanized his name to Tom Carvel when he'd opened an ice cream store in Hartsdale, New York, in 1934. When his Model-A Ford broke down making a delivery, and the truck was unable to pull his ice cream trailer any farther, he watched his hard ice cream start to melt. Luckily for Mr. Carvel, customers seemed to enjoy the softer texture of the not-so-frozen dessert. Two years later he was awarded a patent for the "no air pump" super-low temperature ice cream machine, and soft-serve ice cream was born.

In 1955, a family out

THE SOFT-SERVE SUNDAE BECAME A FAVORITE IN THE 1950S.

SONIC BOOM

In his Top Hat Drive-In in Stillwater, Oklahoma, Troy Smith installed intercom speakers, and trained servers on roller skates to deliver food directly to customers in their cars. Top Hat was the prototype for the Sonic Drive-Ins with, at last count, 2,700 units in 30 states, and six in Mexico. Every year Sonic sells about 18 million gallons of soft-serve ice cream and 78 million cherries. Sonic's choices include hot fudge, strawberry, chocolate, pineapple and peanut butter fudge sundaes.

for a Sunday drive without a Carvel stand in sight might satisfy their sundae yens at a Dairy Queen, which by then had 2,600 locations. J.F. McCullough and his son, Alex, had developed their own version of the continuous-feed soft-serve machine—the invention that gave birth to Dairy Queen. That spark of imagination has exploded into an international company that eventually boasted more than 5,200 stores. During the 1950s and 1960s, Dairy Queens in small towns of the Midwest and South, and most especially Texas, were often a center of social life. They have been referenced as a symbol of life in small-town America in such works as *Walter Benjamin at the Dairy Queen: Reflections at Sixty and Beyond* by Larry McMurtry, *Dairy Queen Days* by Robert Inman, and *Chevrolet Summers, Dairy Queen Nights* by Bob Greene.

THE RECIPES

ROUTE 66 SUNDAE

Wagon train pioneers paved the way for Route 66 by establishing dusty frontier trails to the west from St. Louis in the 1800s. Today's

Dusty Road is a sundae served at the Fair Oaks Pharmacy on Pasadena's Mission Street, part of the original Route 66.

DIP ONE LARGE SCOOP OF VANILLA ICE CREAM AND ONE LARGE SCOOP OF CHOCOLATE ICE CREAM SIDE BY SIDE IN A WIDE SUNDAE BOWL. COVER BOTH SCOOPS WITH CHOCOLATE SYRUP AND DUST WITH MALTED MILK POWDER. FINISH WITH WHIPPED CREAM AND A MARASCHINO ON TOP.

-Fair Oaks Pharmacy, Pasadena, California

POT HOLE SUNDAE

The back roads of Maine are known for potholes the size of Volkswagens.

DIP ONE LARGE SCOOP OF CHOCOLATE ICE CREAM INTO A SUNDAE TULIP. USING A SPOON, CARVE OUT A HOLE IN THE CENTER OF THE SCOOP AND FILL IT WITH HOT FUDGE. COVER OVERALL WITH "BLACKTOP" (CRUSHED CHOCOLATE COOKIES).

-Gifford's Famous Ice Cream, Skohegan, Maine

UNIMPROVED SINCE 1934

Gus Belt founded the first Steak & Shake in the mid-1930s in Normal, Illinois, featuring the gimmick of grinding T-bones, sirloins, and round steaks into burgers right in front of customers who ate at the counter overlooking the kitchen. Today's Steak & Shake restaurants use the slogan, "Unimproved Since 1934." They have revived the Boston Shake, a thick milkshake with a sundae built on top, called a "Sippable Sundae." Choose from Turtle Caramel Nut, Double Chocolate Fudge or Banana Split.

Chapter 17

NUTCRACKER SWEET

*"The Fifties—they seem to have taken place
on a sunny afternoon that asked nothing of you
except a drifting belief in the moment
and its power to satisfy."*

—ELIZABETH HARDWICK

"All Shook Up" played on jukeboxes as a new cultural rhythm gave the American melting pot a good shake, and the whoosh of a whipped cream nozzle was music to the ears. Rock and Roll seemed to re-energize the soda fountain. It was the last era of eating innocence, when a sundae at a place like Tom's Ice Cream Bowl was one of life's great things.

Three scoops in a soup bowl. That's how the former astronaut and retired U.S. senator John Glenn once described his favorite sundae at the popular Zanesville, Ohio, ice cream parlor. Glenn grew up in nearby New Concord and enjoyed many a hot fudge sundae at Tom's.

Those unadulterated bowls of ice cream and syrup still embody carefree days of youth in the long, sleepy summer of Eisenhower's America.

You don't find much in the way of ambiance as you enter through the swinging double doors. Yellow Formica-top tables come with four chrome chairs, upholstered in well-worn green leatherette. Ten matching stools at the counter face three stark mirrors. The floor is industrial terrazzo, and walls are block tiles in a two-tone combination of cream and turquoise. The decor may not be chic but what you do find at Tom's is something more valuable and memorable.

There is hardly an aroma more appetizing than the scent of warm nuts right out of the oven, and that alone would distinguish this shop from less enchanting soda fountains.

At the front of the store, a wooden counter displays fragrant cashews, peanuts, redskins and Spanish nuts, all freshly-roasted for eating by themselves or as sundae toppings.

Tom's does not, praise be, fancy up the ice cream sundae. He doesn't have to. There is no whipped cream here, not a Maraschino cherry in sight. That's the deal, plain and simple. The combination of homemade ice cream and fresh-roasted nuts speaks for itself. As manager Joe Baker tells it, "We don't want anything to get in the way of the nuts."

Baker has been at Tom's since his own high school days, over two decades ago, and he continues to favor wearing a white shirt, bow tie and paper hat while at work. Under his command is a hard-working corps of "clerks," as Tom's soda jerks are called. But Baker, who clearly loves his profession, is happy to tell you he is still the best at what he has trained them to do. "First, we teach each apprentice the art of hand-dipping, and it is indeed an art," he explains. "You have to be fast. You must go down and come up with the right portion in one dip. Only then do you move up to the fountain to make sundaes."

Baker is both passionate and amusing as he coaches his apprentices in "frozen dessert technology."

The fountain, you might correctly infer, is something of an altar at Tom's, and above it hangs the honored portrait of store co-founder Tom Mirgon. Baker can remember Mirgon from his own early clerking days; the

RESPECT FOR OLD AGE

Tom's is nothing but a squalling baby compared to Wittich's Candy, in Circleville, Ohio. Wittich's has been making residents of the Buckeye State happy since 1840, so it's altogether fitting that it has the honor of the Buckeye Sundae. The buckeye is an inedible variety of horse chestnut, but Wittich has gotten around this inconvenience by creating a "buckeye" candy made of chocolate and peanut butter to top its sundae. A Wittich Buckeye Sundae maker covers vanilla ice cream with hot fudge sauce, and chocolate peanut-butter ice cream with peanut-butter sauce. Yum!

Wittich Candy's confection recipes are top secret, but you can approximate the Buckeye Sundae with similar syrups and a chocolate-peanut or chocolate-peanut-butter candy. Better yet, follow your sweet tooth and find your way to Circleville, half an hour's drive south of Columbus.

man was six-foot-four and dispensed ice cream wisdom in a deep, booming voice. He preached cleanliness, good service and fair prices. "If you do that," he would say, "they'll find you no matter where you're located."

Mirgon had studied ice cream-making at the local Hemmer Dairy before he and his cousin, Jack Hemmer, opened Tom's in 1948. In 1953, Mirgon bought out his partner. It was the same year that a customer complained that his sundae overflowed the tulip glass as soon as he put a spoon in it: "Why don't you put this damn thing in a soup bowl so I can eat it?" he is remembered to have asked.

From that day on, Tom's has served its sundaes in the same size bowls as it uses for its soups. Not long after, Mirgon renamed his place Tom's Ice Cream Bowl.

When Mirgon passed the torch to his manager, Bill Sullivan, in 1984, the young man inherited a place that looked like Ozzie and Harriet might walk in at any moment. Sullivan, whose manner is genial yet thoroughly professional, stubbornly refuses to change a thing. "The longer we're here, and the longer we keep it the same, the more of an institution we become," Sullivan told me, with a twinkle in his eyes. "I am certain of that."

THE RECIPES

PEANUT BUTTER SAUCE

1 cup smooth or chunky peanut butter
$^1/_4$ cup light corn syrup

$^1/_2$ cup heavy cream or sweetened condensed milk

COMBINE INGREDIENTS IN A SAUCEPAN OVER LOW HEAT, STIRRING UNTIL WARM AND THICK BUT NOT GUMMY. IF THE SAUCE MUST STAND AND IT THICKENS TOO MUCH, THIN TO DESIRED CONSISTENCY WITH ADDITIONAL CREAM OR CONDENSED MILK. SERVE WARM.

SAUCE CAN BE REFRIGERATED IN AN AIRTIGHT CONTAINER FOR UP TO 3 WEEKS. TO RE-HEAT, MICROWAVE AT 15-SECOND INTERVALS UNTIL WARM. MAKES 1$^1/_2$ CUPS.

TOM'S TRADITIONS

TIN ROOF

Dip 2 large scoops of vanilla ice cream into an 8-ounce soup bowl. Ladle 4 ounces chocolate syrup over the top, and completely cover with one layer of fresh-roasted Spanish peanuts. Place bowl on a saucer and serve.

BLACK AND WHITE

Dip 3 large scoops of vanilla ice cream into an 8-ounce soup bowl. Ladle on 2 ounces of chocolate syrup, then ladle on 2 ounces of marshmallow syrup. Place bowl on a saucer and serve.

–Tom's Ice Cream Bowl, Zanesville, Ohio

Chapter 18

CUSTARD CAPITAL

*"Frozen custard beats the pants off frozen yogurt, and
is about the only thing that gives hand-scooped quality ice cream a run for its money."*

—JON VAN OAST

orn on the family's dairy farm in York, Pennsylvania, in 1893, Archie Kohr became a school teacher and then, to supplement his income, started a home delivery milk business. By 1917, he'd decided to expand the business by selling homemade ice cream to his customers. His ice cream contained eggs (used as an emulsifier) and it was denser than other ice creams. Kohr made the ice cream dense by reconfiguring a gasoline-driven ice cream freezer so that it whipped little air into the dessert.

In the summer of 1919, Archie took the machine and his frozen custard recipe to the Coney Island boardwalk. On the first weekend, using a single machine, he dispensed more than 18,000 cones at a nickel apiece.

It wasn't long before many others had opened frozen custard stands at east coast beaches, but it wasn't until 1933 that frozen custard was introduced to the Midwest at the Chicago World's Fair. From there, it hopped to Wisconsin.

Milwaukee, the largest city in America's dairy state, is home to a diverse population of intrepid, hardworking folks who soften the edges of urban life with Friday night fish fries, Saturday afternoon bratwurst cookouts, and frozen custard practically all the time. Frozen custard has become a Milwaukee specialty; the city is the self-proclaimed "Custard Capital of the World."

The abundant joys of frozen custard have to do with formulation and method of production. By federal law, the custard must contain at least 10% butterfat, at least 1.4% egg-yolk solids (don't worry, they're pasteurized), and very little air. Creaminess is achieved in monstrous machines nicknamed "iron lungs" which slowly churn the cream mixture instead of whipping it.

A quart of frozen custard actually weighs more than a quart of ice cream.

Custard is served at approximately 26 degrees F., while ice cream is usually served at 10 degrees. The higher temperature gives custard a truer taste than ice cream, which tends to numb the taste buds. Frozen custard is luxurious on the tongue; it possesses a velvety quality. Aficionados claim that good custard is creamier than ordinary ice creams and I can't help but agree. Since frozen custard tastes best when eaten fresh, Milwaukee shops make batches of it several times a day. No wonder there are lines in front of the city's custard stands on even cold winter days.

THE RECIPES

ZOMBIE

When Paul Gilles opened his stand in 1938, he had only three items on the menu: hot dogs, root beer and vanilla custard. Since then the menu has expanded to offer sandwiches, side orders, and fancy sundaes like the Zombie.

DIP 3 LARGE SCOOPS OF FROZEN VANILLA CUSTARD SIDE BY SIDE INTO A WIDE SUNDAE DISH. CUT $^1/_2$ BANANA INTO DISKS AND ARRANGE THEM AROUND THE ICE CREAM. COVER ONE SCOOP WITH HOT FUDGE, ONE WITH CRUSHED PINEAPPLE AND ONE WITH CRUSHED STRAWBERRIES. GARNISH EACH SCOOP WITH A DOLLOP OF MARSHMALLOW CRÈME. SPRINKLE CHOCOLATE JIMMIES AND CHOPPED NUTS OVER TOP. PLACE A MARASCHINO CHERRY AT THE TOP OF EACH SCOOP.

–Gilles Frozen Custard, Milwaukee, Wisconsin

SMILE SUNDAE

In a city where custard is king, Elsa Kopp was the queen. She opened the first Kopp's Frozen Custard stand in 1950 as a way to support her family after her husband became disabled. Her son, Karl, is now at the helm. Some dessert fanciers consider Kopp's Custard the best frozen custard in the nation. Food writers Michael and Jane Stern say the vanilla is flawless; in fact, they call it a "vanilla ecstasy experience."

Coat the bottom of a large sundae goblet with chocolate syrup, and dip 3 scoops of frozen vanilla custard inside. Cover with caramel syrup. Garnish with marshmallow créme and sprinkle jumbo peanuts over top. Drizzle chocolate syrup over all.

–Kopp's Frozen Custard, Milwaukee, Wisconsin

DUSTY TRAIL

Leon Schneider's place was the inspiration for Arnold's drive-in on TV's Happy Days. Milwaukee custard culture is alive and well at Leon's Frozen Custard Drive-In, where the custard is churned in the front window, then scooped by blue-uniformed attendants into cones, dishes, and sundaes such as the Dusty Trail.

Dip one large scoop of frozen chocolate custard into a sundae tulip. Cover with marshmallow créme and sprinkle chocolate jimmies over top.

–Leon's Frozen Custard Drive-In, Milwaukee, Wisconsin

FAT CAT SUNDAE

Milwaukee natives, Michael and Kim Schmidt, named their version of a neighborhood custard stand for their pet.

Dip one large scoop of frozen chocolate custard into a sundae tulip. Cover with chocolate syrup and sprinkle with crushed Oreos. Garnish with marshmallow créme.

–Bella's Fat Cat, Milwaukee, Wisconsin

Chapter 19

SUNDAE IN NEW YORK

"When the Woolworth's hot-fudge-sundae switch goes on, then I know I really have something."

—ANDY WARHOL

ndy Warhol, who grew up in Pittsburgh, Pennsylvania, fantasizing about the bright lights of Manhattan, once suggested that it would be glamorous to be reincarnated as a great big ring on Liz Taylor's finger. By 1955, he made it to New York where he discovered a glorified coffeehouse called Serendipity 3 before the world discovered him. At Serendipity 3, he sipped espresso and devoured sundaes and paid for them with his drawings. Serendipity's ice cream sundaes became iconic subjects in some sketches.

MUCH BESIDES GLORIOUS SUNDAES IS FOR SALE AT SERENDIPITY 3.

HICKS AND FLICKS

*B*efore Serendipity there was Hicks. For three-quarters of a century, Hicks did its best to slow down frenzied adults, some accompanied by clamoring children, in its tranquil aqua and cotton-candy-pink setting. You could order a Supreme Flaming Robin Rose Glow—apple, orange, pineapple, banana, grapes, and strawberries with ice creams of various flavors on top of a slice of pound cake, or you could direct the fountain-master to construct a sundae of your own fantasy. Some Hicks' fans wax rhapsodic over the memory of one obliging fountain chief: Mr. Jennings. If not for Mr. Jennings, many city children would never have known that dreams and sundaes are the same thing.

Some of those kids grew up to become patrons of a dim cavern called The Flick. The Flick hired aspiring actresses, dressed them in thigh-high, black net stockings and low-cut leotards, and sent them out to deliver sundaes with names like the Mission Impossible—Burgundy cherry, rum raisin, and eggnog ice creams oozing with butterscotch, marshmallow, hot fudge, crushed pineapple and whipped cream. At 9 p.m., midnight and 3 a.m., the lights went down, and you were treated to "flicks"—old comedies of W.C. Fields, Laurel and Hardy and Charlie Chaplin.

As for the café, it's much the same as when Warhol frequented it, which is to say it's not low key. Serendipity is swanked out with Tiffany lamps, Victorian posters and a multitude of other adornments. "Everything's for sale," quips owner Steven Bruce, while watering the potted palms. "Well, almost everything." Bruce dressed windows at Macy's before dreaming up his campy cosmos.

To mark its 50th anniversary in 2004, Serendipity offered a remarkable foot-tall sundae with five scoops of rich Tahitian vanilla ice cream, topped off with 23K edible gold leaf, chocolates made from cocoa beans found only on the Venezuelan coast, and an array of exotic fruits and Beluga caviar sweetened and infused with passion fruit, orange liqueur and Armagnac. Each sundae took the staff a full hour to create. The result was served in a Baccarat crystal goblet accompanied by a gold-plated spoon. Named the Golden Opulence Sundae, it was listed on Serendipity's menu at $1,000.

"There's no evidence of a more expensive sundae anywhere else in the world," said a representative from *Guinness Book of World Records*.

THE RECIPES

SAND TART SUNDAE

A traditional Southern-recipe cookie supports one of Serendipity's oldest and most beloved sundaes.

SAND TART COOKIES

$^1/_2$ cup butter, softened	$^1/_2$ teaspoon salt
$^3/_4$ cup confectioners sugar	1 teaspoon baking powder
$^1/_4$ cup brown sugar	$1^1/_2$ cups all-purpose flour
2 eggs, separated	1 cup almonds, crushed
1 tablespoon milk	1 tablespoon granulated sugar
$^1/_2$ teaspoon vanilla extract	$^1/_2$ teaspoon cinnamon

CREAM BUTTER AND SUGARS. ADD EGG YOLKS, MILK AND VANILLA AND BEAT UNTIL LIGHT. ADD SIFTED DRY INGREDIENTS AND MIX WELL. CHILL DOUGH FOR $1^1/_2$ HOURS. ON A LIGHTLY FLOURED SURFACE, ROLL DOUGH TO $^1/_4$-INCH THICKNESS AND CUT WITH 4-INCH STAR-SHAPED COOKIE CUTTER. PLACE ON GREASED COOKIE SHEETS AND SPRINKLE CRUSHED ALMONDS OVER TOP. BRUSH WITH UNBEATEN EGG WHITES; SPRINKLE WITH 1 TABLESPOON GRANULATED SUGAR AND THE CINNAMON. BAKE IN 375-DEGREE OVEN FOR 14 MINUTES. MAKES 24 COOKIES.

PLACE A SAND TART COOKIE ON A PLATTER, AND DIP ONE LARGE SCOOP OF COFFEE ICE CREAM OVER TOP. COVER WITH HOT FUDGE. GARNISH WITH WHIPPED CREAM AND SPRINKLE WITH CRUMBLED SAND TART COOKIES.

-Serendipity 3, New York, New York

IT STARTED IN BROOKLYN

Brooklyn natives John and Rick Russo started selling homemade ice cream and ices on Coney Island Avenue in 1998. The ice cream flavors and specialty sundaes, dreamed up by Rick's wife, Carmen Barrios, propelled "Uncle Louie G" into the big time, with, at last count, 40 locations from New York to Florida. "Brooklyn Cheesecake" ice cream is made with chunks of local cheesecake from legendary Junior's of Brooklyn. No wonder Uncle Louie G's ice cream was recently named Official Ice Cream of the borough.

BROOKLYN BRIDGE

Dip one large scoop of cookies & cream ice cream and one large scoop of chocolate fudge brownie ice cream side by side in a wide sundae dish. Cover the cookies & cream with crushed pineapple and the chocolate fudge brownie with crushed strawberries. Ladle a generous portion of hot fudge over all. Garnish with whipped cream and rainbow sprinkles.

UPPER EAST SIDE

Dip 2 large scoops of cappuccino chunk ice cream into a tall goblet. Cover with hot fudge and crunchies (crumbled cookies). Garnish with whipped cream and place a cherry at the top.

–Uncle Louis G, Brooklyn

Chapter 20

THE BIG CHILL

*"What really distinguishes ice cream parlors
is their atmosphere, and therein lies the difference
between a sundae that satisfies the palate
and one that satisfies the soul."*

—Fran R. Schumer

It's not often that New Yorkers cry into their ice cream sundaes, but it was such sweet sorrow when faithful patrons had to face life without Schrafft's.

Opened in 1906, Schrafft's Ice Cream Parlor grew into a sprawling dynasty of 52 restaurants. Boston hosted six; Newark, White Plains, Syracuse and Philadelphia each claimed one; the others were all in New York City.

The typical Schrafft's boasted decorous chandeliers, cherry-veneer paneling, upright chairs that encouraged perfect posture and a soda fountain. Even at the fountain, its sundae goblets were carefully set on lacy paper doilies. Schrafft's leading dessert was the Broadway Sundae, made with chocolate ice cream topped with hot fudge and toasted almonds and pecans.

In the 1960s, Schrafft's business spun downward and its executives asked Andy Warhol to design a commercial that would update its image. Warhol's TV spot opened with a red dot in the darkness that lands atop what is revealed as an ice cream sundae, exploding in psychedelic colors.

The voice-over described this as "Yummy Schrafft's vanilla ice cream in two groovy heaps, with three ounces of mind-blowing chocolate sauce undulating within a mountain of pure whipped cream, topped with a pulsating maraschino cherry, served in a bowl as big as a boat."

After the last Schrafft's closed in 1985, Tom Wolfe eulogized the restaurant: "Schrafft's was not exactly the most prestigious place for a woman to eat. But eating at Schrafft's did have a certain secret beauty to it: the much underestimated beauty of American Comfort. The ladies' typical meal at Schrafft's was a cheeseburger, coffee and a sundae. But such sundaes!

Sundaes with towers of ice cream and nuts and sauces and fudge and maraschino cherries of a quality and buttery beauty such as the outside world has never dreamed of!"

THE RECIPES

THE BEST
OF SCHRAFFT'S

William Schrafft Schulz of Boston is heir to the Schrafft's legacy by virtue of his great-grandfather's marriage to Louise Schrafft, a daughter of William F. Schrafft, the company founder. Will is the keeper of the original family recipes for butterscotch and hot fudge sauces, which are offered here, with his gracious permission.

You may, however, need more than these two recipes to replicate the pleasure of sundae-eating at genteel Schrafft's. It's recommended that ladies wear hats to the table and that gentlemen help these hat-wearing ladies into their chairs.

HOT FUDGE SAUCE

1 tablespoon unsweetened cocoa powder	2 ounces unsweetened chocolate, chopped
1 cup sugar	1 teaspoon vanilla extract
3/4 cup heavy cream	Pinch of salt
1/4 cup light corn syrup	Few drops of malt vinegar
2 tablespoons unsalted butter	

IN A HEAVY MEDIUM SAUCEPAN OVER MEDIUM HEAT, WHISK TOGETHER THE COCOA, SUGAR, AND 1/4 CUP OF THE HEAVY CREAM UNTIL SMOOTH, ABOUT 2 MINUTES. STIR IN THE CORN SYRUP, BUTTER, UNSWEETENED CHOCOLATE BITS AND REMAINING 1/2 CUP HEAVY CREAM, AND BRING TO A BOIL. REMOVE FROM THE HEAT AND STIR IN THE VANILLA, SALT AND VINEGAR.

SAUCE MAY BE REFRIGERATED IN AN AIRTIGHT CONTAINER FOR UP TO 3 WEEKS. TO REHEAT, SET OVER A DOUBLE BOILER, WHISKING VIGOROUSLY. IF REHEATING OVER DIRECT HEAT, USE VERY LOW FLAME, AND BE CAREFUL NOT TO LET THE SAUCE BUBBLE OR BURN. MAKES 2 CUPS.

A Schrafft's Dining Room Standing Ready for the Businessmen and Hatted Ladies Who Lunched There.

BUTTERSCOTCH SAUCE

1 cup packed light brown sugar
$^1/_2$ cup light corn syrup
6 tablespoons ($^3/_4$ stick) unsalted
   butter

$^1/_8$ tablespoon salt
$^1/_2$ cup heavy cream
$^1/_2$ teaspoon vanilla extract

IN A HEAVY MEDIUM SAUCEPAN, COMBINE THE BROWN SUGAR, CORN SYRUP, BUTTER, AND SALT. BRING TO A BOIL, STIRRING CONSTANTLY, OVER MEDIUM HEAT, AND COOK FOR ONE MINUTE. TURN OFF THE HEAT AND STIR IN THE CREAM, THEN STIR IN THE VANILLA. ALLOW TO COOL SLIGHTLY (MIXTURE WILL BE VERY HOT). SERVE WARM.

INTO THE SUNSET

Bob Farrell, the founder of the Oregon-based Farrell's Ice Cream Parlour chain, grew up in Brooklyn. "In Brooklyn, there were little ice cream stores on every corner— fountain, candies, little café tables and stools," Farrell once told an interviewer. "I love hot fudge sundaes. I could die for hot fudge sundaes."

Farrell's biggest sundae was the Portland Zoo, which fed 10 to 15 people and was ceremoniously delivered to the table on a hospital stretcher doubling as a tray.

In 1975, Farrell sold his 150-store empire to the Marriott Corporation, which withdrew from the restaurant business seven years later and disbanded the chain.

Many of Bob Farrell's customers wanted to have their sundaes and their cakes, too. These two recipes date from the mid-'60s .

TWO ON A BLANKET

Dip one large scoop each of vanilla and chocolate ice cream side by side on a slice of pound cake. Ladle hot fudge sauce over the vanilla and marshmallow syrup over the chocolate. Garnish with whipped cream, sprinkle with chopped mixed nuts and place a maraschino cherry at the top of each scoop.

APPLE PANDOWDY

Dip 2 large scoops of vanilla ice cream into a tall goblet. Cover with hot sliced baked apples and crumbles of crispy-baked pie dough. Garnish with whipped cream, dust with nutmeg and place a cherry at the top.

Chapter 21

FRENCH
CONNECTION

"Ice-cream is exquisite—
what a pity it isn't illegal."

—Voltaire

There has, it seems, always been a struggle to elevate American cuisine, to make it more sophisticated—in other words, to make it as French as possible. For some, the ice cream sundae is out of place in a setting of linen tablecloths, polished silver and crystal glassware. If the sundae were to reach that level, they must have surmised, it needed a fancy-pants pseudonym.

The French have a word for everything, and in their vocabulary, *parfait* means "perfect." It's the name they give to a dessert of semi-frozen mousse with a variety of flavorings. With typical American bravado, we have muddled the term and applied it to dolled-up sundaes, usually constructed in an alternating sequence of ingredients. The most notable difference between the ice cream sundae and an American parfait is the dish in which it's placed. While a sundae is most often served in a wide-mouth goblet, the parfait is layered in a tall, ice-cream-soda style glass.

In Buffalo, New York, a spacious hybrid of candy shop and ice cream fountain was the 1927 vision of George and Molly Kaiser and their architect, G. Morton Wolfe, who claimed inspiration from Parisian confectionary salons. In any case, the flamboyant Parkside Candy Company was a match for the optimism and braggadocio of Buffalo's emergence as an industrial center. That day has come and is long gone, but it survives in Parkside. True, the years have not been kind to its exterior. But, like an aging beauty, some great features hang on.

The must-be-seen-to-be-believed setting suggests a gigantic carousel, surrounded by lustrous solid walnut candy showcases, which display candies like brilliant jewels. Three chandeliers dangle from the whimsical and colorful domed ceiling, bathing the assembler of ice cream sundaes as well as Parkside patrons in a warm glow. Meanwhile, the aromatic cocoa butter in the candies perfumes the entire room with the scent of chocolate.

Ann Marie Ranger, the energetic fountain manager at Parkside recounts her first visit. "My folks took us to see *The Sound of Music* at the Granada," she recalls, "then, after the movie, we walked across the street to Parkside Candy, with everyone still humming *do re mi*. I will never forget it."

Her parfait composition is a stylized mosaic of colors, overlapping but distinct, alternating with egg-shaded French vanilla ice cream in massive Anchor-Hocking goblets. The French would recognize Ranger's virtuosity if not her dessert. To anyone interested in the language of food, Parkside Candy's confident concoctions cross any linguistic barriers. No wonder folks in Buffalo have a special place in their hearts for Parkside.

THE RECIPES

C'EST PARFAIT

*T*hese are the time-tested parfait rules: Start by putting the syrup at the bottom of the glass, use ice cream that has become slightly soft and push down hard every time you add an ice cream layer. This forces the liquid up in the glass, creating the ripple effect that is the signature of a well-made parfait.

STRAWBERRY PARFAIT INGREDIENTS

Vanilla ice cream
Strawberry Topping (recipe below)

Whipped cream
Maraschino cherries

STRAWBERRY TOPPING

1 cup strawberry concentrate
1 cup frozen unsweetened straw-
  berries, thawed

1 cup Simple Syrup (recipe below)
1 teaspoon lemon juice

To make the topping, Parkside Candy uses a strawberry concentrate that has been produced by Buffalo jam makers, Henry and Henry, since 1899. But you can substitute a high-quality supermarket jam.

Mix strawberries with concentrate, then stir in Simple Syrup and lemon juice. This recipe is enough to top 8 to 10 parfaits.

SIMPLE SYRUP

1 cup water   2 tablespoons light corn syrup
1 cup sugar

Combine water, sugar and corn syrup in a saucepan and bring to a boil, stirring until sugar is dissolved. Simmer undisturbed for 2 minutes. Cool to room temperature before adding to other strawberry topping ingredients.

Alternate topping and ice cream in a tall (20-ounce) goblet. Begin by filling a 2-ounce ladle with strawberry topping, and drop the topping to the bottom of the glass. Insert one large scoop of French vanilla ice cream, then add another 2 ounces of the topping. Dip a second large scoop of vanilla and add 2 more ounces of topping. Dip a third scoop of vanilla and cover with strawberry topping. Garnish with whipped cream and place a maraschino cherry on top.

–Parkside Candy, Buffalo, New York

Two views of the Parkside Ice Cream Parlor

Chapter 22

FROZEN IN TIME

"The harvest of old age is the recollection and abun-dance of blessings previously secured."

—Cicero

*I*n Missouri, the sundae has been pronounced "sunduh" since way back when. So, how do you explain it? "Sunday is the day you go to church," says Andrew Karandzieff, "and a 'sunduh' is what you eat after you go to church."

He ought to know. Andrew, along with brothers Michael and Thomas, perpetuate the family legacy at a revered St. Louis relic called Crown Candy Kitchen. This candy and ice cream parlor has stood on the corner of St. Louis Avenue and 14th Street for over nine decades.

Just after the turn of the last century, a young Greek named Harry Karandzieff brought confectionery skills with him to St. Louis. At first he worked at a shoe factory for $3 a day but after two years he found a modest space to pursue his candy dreams. Before long, his establishment became known for both its hand-rolled sweets and ice cream sundaes.

BEING JULIA

*"L*ife itself is the proper binge," said Julia Child, the late grand dame of American cuisine. She revolutionized cooking in the United States with her cooking school, cookbooks and television shows. Ms. Child spent her later years in Montecito, California, often dining at Lucky's, where she could have one of her beloved turtle sundaes, layered with caramel, fudge and buttery pecans.

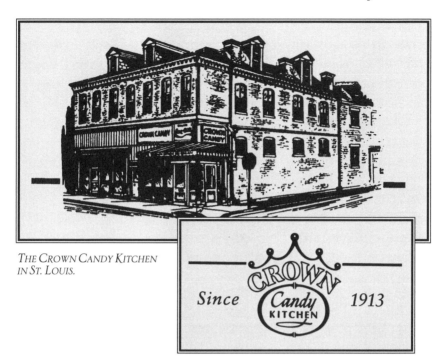

THE CROWN CANDY KITCHEN
IN ST. LOUIS.

If memory is not playing tricks on the Karandzieff clan, the store has been open every day since 1913, seven days a week, save for a few weeks following a fire on the day after Christmas, 1983.

Sweeter times begin the moment you step inside. Authentic Coca-Cola memorabilia hangs on the walls for decoration. A few rays of late-morning sun accentuate the aged, off-white booths. They are exactly as they've always been, except for the backs. When the ladies who lunch on sundaes in St. Louis complained that they were neither able to see nor be seen due to the booths' high backs, they were dragged out, sawed down and repainted over one weekend (the booths, not the ladies).

The Karandzieffs, grandsons three, work hand in hand, energized, they say, by the dedication of those who came before them. Tom is the short-order cook who feeds a small army every day; Andy produces daily batches of ice cream, and takes special pride in his snow-white vanilla; Mike dances behind the counter, skillfully scooping Andy's ice cream into cones, malts and sundaes.

The menu offers ice cream concoctions in three defiantly ancient modes, long since vanished from most American soda fountains. A sundae is ice cream and syrup, that's it; a Newport includes whipped cream and nuts; a Deluxe adds more flavors of ice cream and/or syrups.

The single greatest thing to eat at Crown Candy Kitchen is the

Crown Sundae. It's the Holy Grail of ice cream sundaes, served in a generous goblet, and the closest most of us will ever come to perfection. Each one arrives with its combination of house-made ingredients oozing over the edge, hot fudge competing with caramel sauce for your attention, not to mention the butter-roasted pecans.

This sacrosanct sundae has never gone out of style. It has always been made in exactly the same way, and it commands unyielding loyalty from customers. It's not really unique. It's not hard to make. It's not particularly beautiful, but it has a little of all these things, and perhaps that's why it satisfies a lot of different people.

THE RECIPES

CROWN SUNDAE

Dip 2 large scoops of vanilla ice cream into a tall sundae goblet. Cover with 2 ounces of hot fudge sauce and 2 ounces of caramel sauce. Sprinkle butter-roasted pecans over the top.

FIRE CHIEF SPECIAL

Dip 2 large scoops of vanilla ice cream side by side into a wide sundae bowl. Cover one scoop with chocolate syrup, the other with crushed strawberries. Place round slices of bananas around the ice cream. Garnish with whipped cream, sprinkle with chopped pecans and chopped cashews, and place a maraschino cherry at the top.

–*Crown Candy Kitchen*, St. Louis, Missouri

Chapter 23

SUNDAE HEAVEN IN CHICAGO

"A hot fudge sundae and a trashy novel is my idea of heaven."

—Barbara Walters

ooth Five, the L-shaped, gold-vinyl seat in the corner of a beloved Chicago sweet shop, is where George Poulos proposed to Margie Michaels in 1932. Depending on your point of view, it's either cluttered and cramped or intimate and romantic, but, in either case, it's where the story begins. She was the pretty young carpenter's daughter who worked at Security Candies, and, almost as soon as she said "yes" to George, its owner, the name of the store was changed to Margie's Candies.

Chicago is a city that can be resistant to change, so when it comes to old establishments more than a few of the genuine articles survive. Margie's Candies has stood like a rock at the edge of the Bucktown neighborhood since Poulos and his father opened for business in 1921. Today, Margie's is a quirky combination of restaurant, ice cream parlor, candy shop and toy store—a place of comforting, nourishing tradition, only slightly more commodious than a phone booth.

There is nothing about the unassuming storefront that might tip a casual visitor to the fact that he or she has found the single best place for ice cream sundaes in the city. But step inside and pick up a menu, choose from 2-dip to 25-dip concoctions, and—oh, Lord!—you'll know you're in sundae heaven.

In the early days, Margie Poulos labored as a candy dipper in the morning, then as a waitress when the store opened. Standing just over five feet tall, braided hair tied back in a bun, and always dressed in floral print dress with a starched white apron, she was admired by practically everyone who knew her. Margie was very proud that the store carried her name, and she worked tirelessly to make it better.

When World War II came, her husband left to defend the country, and

Margie was left to defend the store. By day, she coped with sugar rationing and chocolate shortages; at night, she took business classes. During the war, she also traveled to New York to attend cooking and candy-making classes, remodeled the store interior, and cared for her son. Her husband returned home to find that sales had doubled.

There are no wimpy sundaes at Margie's. You need to think twice before ordering a meal before dessert; this is the kind of place where a hot fudge sundae is dinner. A huge portion of ice cream is accompanied by a stainless steel urn filled with rich, deep, dark, bittersweet hot fudge sauce–more than you will ever use; but erring on the side of generosity is another tradition here.

Margie offers many large, delicious sundaes, but how can anything compare to the likes of the Jumbo Fudge Atomic Sundae? A large white plastic shell is piled high with rich vanilla ice cream, then covered in a lattice of candy-dipping chocolate. Watch one being made and you'll see the warm fudge being precisely drizzled, then hardening when it hits the ice cream. The fudge-covered ice cream is then made to all but disappear under an enormous cloud of whipped cream, chopped nuts and a cherry.

The famous and infamous have been dropping in since the days

MARGIE'S CANDIES ON A SUMMER DAY.

when Al Capone sat in a corner booth and kept his eyes on the plate-glass windows and door. He must have also noticed the old wooden cash drawer, because one day he had a mechanical cash register delivered to the store. The ornate black register still sits on a shelf behind the counter. Walt Disney once celebrated a birthday here. Michael Jackson brought an entourage for sundaes and stayed all night. Even the Beatles came for sundaes, sneaking into Margie's after their 1965 concert in Comiskey Park.

If the ice cream enterprise called Margie's Candies is an example, great big sundaes are in no danger of becoming extinct. There is one difference between now and the old days, though. Margie Poulos is gone. In 1995, she spent nearly a whole day, sitting in Booth Five, tying bows on 200 Easter candy baskets. The next day she passed away at age 80.

Margie Poulos is the patron saint of the ice cream sundae in Chicago. She dedicated her life to the store that bears her name, and the city is richer for it.

THE RECIPES

BUCKTOWN SPECIAL

Dip 2 large scoops of vanilla ice cream into a wide shell. Surround the ice cream with round slices of banana, then cover with hot fudge sauce and marshmallow syrup. Garnish with whipped cream and place a maraschino cherry at the top. Two vanilla wafers come on the side.

PINA COLADA SUNDAE

Dip 4 large scoops of vanilla ice cream into a wide shell. Surround the ice cream with round slices of banana and bite-size chunks of fresh pineapple. Garnish with whipped cream and place a maraschino at the top. Serve with an urn of hot fudge sauce and 2 vanilla wafers.

—Margie's Candies, Chicago, Illinois

MERRY-GO-ROUND SUNDAE

What goes 'round comes 'round in the Chicago suburb of Oak Park. In 1931, Danish immigrant Hans Petersen moved his ice cream shop to Chicago Avenue (in what's known as the Frank Lloyd Wright historical district), and it has been serving whimsical sundaes at the same location ever since. Petersen appreciated loyalty; his will, executed in 1963, left his establishment to five employees, who had been with him at least 30 years.

DIP ONE LARGE SCOOP OF VANILLA ICE CREAM ONTO THE CENTER OF A FLAT SUNDAE DISH. COVER THE ICE CREAM WITH CHOCOLATE SYRUP AND STICK A PAPER UMBRELLA IN THE TOP. SURROUND WITH ANIMAL CRACKERS FOR THE RIDE.

–Petersen's Old-Fashioned Ice Creams, Oak Park, Illinois

MUDDLE SUNDAE

*a*t age nine, James Papageorge was a successful transatlantic stowaway who then made his way to Chicago, where he found work as a soda jerk. Papageorge saved his pennies, and in 1920 he bought the ice cream parlor nestled next to the Gayety Theater on Chicago's South Side. The theater closed years ago, but Gayety's Chocolates and Ice Cream thrives in the hands of the Papageorge family.

ONE LARGE SCOOP OF VANILLA-BEAN ICE CREAM INTO A SUNDAE TULIP. COVER THE ICE CREAM WITH CARAMEL SAUCE. GARNISH WITH WHIPPED CREAM AND SPRINKLE WITH WHOLE ROASTED PECANS. SERVE WITH A SMALL PITCHER OF HOT FUDGE SAUCE.

–Gayety's Chocolates and Ice Cream, Chicago, Illinois

Chapter 24

MOTHER OF ALL SUNDAES

"We do not get ice-cream everywhere, and so, when we do, we are apt to dissipate to excess."
—MARK TWAIN, *INNOCENTS ABROAD*

The jam-packed ice cream sundae can stand as a metaphor for American bigness and indulgence. We have more of most good things than most other places, and there are practically no bounds to size in either the portions at our tables or in other exaggerations in our national life. As *New York Times* columnist Maureen Dowd once wrote, "We don't have limits. We have liberties… We are America."

That doesn't mean that Americans won't accept curtailment of pleasures in times of crisis. We've accepted sacrifices, including culinary ones, since colonial rebels dumped tea in Boston harbor. Nonetheless, Americans, by nature and fortunate circumstance, are generous; we are not stingy with others, and unnecessary self-denial is not part of our national character.

In some ways, our national propensities were foreshadowed by the Revolutionary general, Israel Putnam. He was a courageous, colorful individual whose biggest appetite was for liberty; it's fitting that one of his descendants runs a sundae extravaganza in his very birthplace.

As soon as Putnam received word of the "shots heard 'round the world," those igniting the skirmishes at Concord and Lexington, he dropped his plow, unyoked his team and without so much as a change of clothes rode off to join the battle.

Two months later, he led a brigade at Bunker Hill. As a swarm of British advanced in their scarlet coats, Putnam had his men lie in wait to attack until the last possible second, since they held precious little ammunition. He issued the now-famous command, "Men, you are all marksmen—don't one of you fire until you see the whites of their eyes!" Then, with a deafening roar amid plumes of gunpowder smoke, the ragtag colonials drove back the British.

The original Putnam homestead in Danvers, Massachusetts, stands transformed into a candy factory and ice cream parlor. An historical marker announces you are in the right place when you drive up to the clapboard saltbox housing Putnam Pantry.

Ten generations removed from "Old Put," Galo Putnam Emerson became a folk hero to ice cream lovers when he invented the sundae bar back in 1958. Emerson is the proprietor and head confectioner of Putnam Pantry, started by his father.

Charm exudes from all directions in cheerful Putnam Pantry: Display cases and tables are laden with so

many delicious-looking candies that it's hard to make a pick. The hodgepodge of replica Colonial furniture mixed with vintage soda fountain furniture is charming. Above one fireplace is a portrait of Gen. Putnam himself.

Yet the heart of the enterprise is the 14-foot stainless-steel sundae bar, offering 16 ice creams, three frozen yogurts and orange or rainbow sherbets. You start by selecting a bowl—the sizes are junior, regular or large; the large bowl is silver in color.

You proceed, unrestrained, to increasingly difficult decisions, such as whether to ladle on hot fudge, hot butterscotch, hot penuche (brown sugar fudge sauce) or dark chocolate sauce. Emerson's experience and expertise as a candy maker has much to do with the excellence of embellishments. Then, what will it be? Sliced strawberries, crushed pineapple or coconut? Chopped walnuts or peanuts? Macaroon crunch or crushed Oreos? Whipped cream or marshmallow syrup? A sprinkle of jimmies or not? You are creating your own vision of what an ice cream sundae should be.

Throw caution to the wind, but don't forget the cherry on top. There is little room for miscalculation with only one pass-through allowed.

I could see that this place is all about overload as I watched five giggling 30-something girlfriends storm in for a don't-let's-count-calories visit to the sundae bar. The first in line quizzed the server. "Is it all you can eat? Can you go up six times?"

"I need this like I need a hole in the head!" declared the second, as she loaded strawberries and hot fudge atop her high-butterfat vanilla ice cream. Her whipped cream was piled so high that the sundae's cherry appeared to sway from side to side in the goo. Another woman seemed to choose toppings by color, as though she was accessorizing.

The sundae bar brings out gluttony in almost everyone, Emerson concedes. "People really pile on the toppings," he explains, "so we give them a plate underneath to catch whatever falls off."

It probably comes as news to no one: The most fattening thing you can put into an ice cream sundae is a spoon. Thankfully, there is still a place where it is permissible to load up on calories in full public view. God bless the Putnam Pantry.

THE RECIPES

WHEELBARROW SUNDAE

The Mortensen legacy began in 1915 with Elmer Mortensen who delivered milk door to door by horse and wagon. Today, the Mortensen family makes some of the best homemade-style ice cream in Connecticut at their shop on Berlin Turnpike in Newington.

Mortensen's claim to fame is the Wheelbarrow Sundae, a four-cubic-foot wheelbarrow filled with 200 scoops of ice cream. The menu says you can keep the wheelbarrow, but you need to place your order a week in advance.

DIP 200 LARGE SCOOPS OF ICE CREAM (APPROXIMATELY 40 QUARTS) INTO A FOIL-LINED, FULL-SIZE WHEELBARROW. TOP WITH $1/2$ GALLON EACH OF CHOCOLATE SYRUP AND CRUSHED STRAWBERRIES. PEEL AND SPLIT ONE LARGE

BUNCH OF BANANAS AND PLACE AROUND THE BASE OF THE ICE CREAM. GARNISH WITH $^1/_2$ GALLON OF WHIPPED HEAVY CREAM, AND PLACE ONE PINT OF MARASCHINO CHERRIES AT THE TOP.

–Mortensen's, Newington, Connecticut

PIG DINNER SUNDAE

Excess, thy name is "Pig Dinner Sundae." If you finish this extravagance on the premises, you get a button that says, "I made a pig of myself at Sherman's."

LINE A WOODEN CONTAINER SHAPED LIKE A PIG'S TROUGH WITH WAXED PAPER. SPLIT ONE LARGE BANANA LENGTHWISE AND PLACE ON THE BOTTOM OF THE TROUGH. ADD ONE LARGE SCOOP EACH OF VANILLA, CHOCOLATE, STRAWBERRY AND BUTTER PECAN ICE CREAM ON TOP. LADLE 2 OUNCES EACH OF CHOCOLATE SAUCE, MARSHMALLOW SYRUP, CRUSHED STRAWBERRIES AND CRUSHED PINEAPPLE OVER THE SCOOPS. GARNISH WITH WHIPPED CREAM, SPRINKLE WITH CHOPPED MIXED NUTS AND PLACE 5 MARASCHINO CHERRIES ACROSS THE TOP.

–Sherman's Dairy Bar, South Haven, Michigan

Chapter 25

LOVIN' SPOONFULS

"You can have everything you want,
just eat it in very small portions."

—MIREILLE GUILIANO

This bit of wisdom above from the author of *French Woman Don't Get Fat* has particular pertinence to our land of plenty, although some of us honor it in the breach. Sundaes, any way you scoop them, are beloved—yet at any given time of year one-third of Americans are trying to shed pounds.

This contradiction prompted the novel idea of Rosy and Rich Bergin, who have conspired against culinary dogma to create a dessert that cleaves to a single piece of tableware. Think small. That's what they do at the Shark and Rose, a cozy restaurant and pub in San Jose, California, where a bas-

---

NO SHIRT, NO SHOES, NO PANTS—NO SERVICE

So reads the sign at the entrance to Ed Debevic's Short Order in Chicago, where servers dressed as bobby-soxers, greasers, and cheerleaders sing, dance and take your order. This parody of a 1950s diner features the World's Smallest Hot Fudge Sundae, a dessert with a one-ounce scoop of vanilla and a drizzle of hot fudge. The sundae comes to the table in an ornate, eye-wash-cup-size, sherry-glass-shaped goblet, accompanied by a tiny spoon. Once customers down the sundae in a swallow or two, they're welcome to take the logo-emblazoned goblet home as a souvenir.

tion of foodies have embraced the itsy-bitsy inspiration called Soup Spoon Sundae.

"My customers can't say 'no' to a dessert this size, no matter how full they are after dinner," Rosy Bergin explains. "It's just one spoonful!"

This dessert is never shared. A little of what you fancy does you good, it is said, but how many of us can stop after just a little ice cream? Apparently, many Shark and Rose patrons can. Still, there are a few who order second helpings of the splendid little sundae with the wincingly cute name.

Rosy, who stands nearly six feet tall, is a veteran of five years on the Women's Professional Beach Volleyball tour. She is still on the run, sharing management responsibilities for three restaurants with her husband.

While the Soup Spoon Sundae may have been Rich's bright idea, it was left to Rosy to

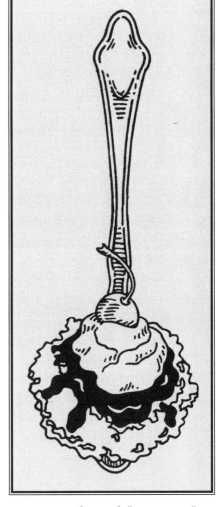

figure out how to put it together. "It was a pain in the neck," Rosy says. "No one could find a commercial dipper small enough." She experimented until she found that a restaurant bouillon spoon would work.

The perfect solution rested on the ice cream-scooping technique Rosy had learned when she was 15 and working at a local ice cream shop. To make the sundae, she rolled the bouillon spoon across the inside of a tub of vanilla ice cream. A seamless motion allowed for a bit of air in the middle, as she got a strip of ice cream to curl around itself until she had formed a scoop that fit into the spoon's shallow bowl.

Rosy decided to keep the perfect mini-scoop in the spoon, so she drizzled on chocolate and then dabbed a very restrained dollop of whipped cream on top. Each Soup Spoon Sundae is served on its own white plate.

HOW TO ADD CALORIES TO YOGURT

*F*rank D. Hickingbotham hated yogurt, until his wife got him to try the Daniel Brackeen's frozen yogurt sold at Neiman-Marcus in Dallas. After his first bite he exclaimed, "This can't be yogurt!"

The result was Hickingbotham's store, This Can't Be Yogurt, in the Market Place shopping center in Little Rock, Arkansas. Twenty years later, TCBY (which now stands for The Country's Best Yogurt) has 3,000 locations, including some abroad.

TCBY Enterprises reports its most-requested toppings are:

1. Hot Fudge
2. Strawberries
3. Non-fat Hot Fudge
4. Walnuts in Syrup
5. Chocolate Chip Cookie Dough
6. M&Ms Plain Chocolate Candies
7. Hot Cherry Topping
8. Oreo Cookies
9. Hot Caramel
10. Gummy Bear Candies

Don't look now, but a server just entered the dining room holding aloft a tray of Soup Spoon Sundaes intended for a party of six. As she zeroes in on the target table, diners at other tables in the busy room take note. When she presents the diminutive desserts, all six spoons on a single oyster plate, everyone at the table breaks into applause.

The server gives each diner a small dessert plate. As she circles the table, presenting the sundae platter to each diner, a tanned blonde, the paradigm of thin, looks absolutely giddy. But the fellow next to her appears slightly discomfited. He must be thinking: *Is that all there is?*

AN AMERICAN ICON

Everything about Kate Smith was outsized, including Miss Smith herself. She recorded almost 3,000 songs in the 1940s and '50s, but was best known for her rendition of <u>God Bless America</u>. In the 1960s she dieted and shed 90 pounds. But she told <u>The New York Times</u> that giving up "real chocolate fudge sundaes" wasn't worth it, and began eating her way back up to her comfort zone.

There is a pause when each dessert eater has his or her spoon by the handle. Two customers stare at their desserts for a second, then at each other, perhaps considering proper etiquette. Emily Post never thought of this one. Left on their own, half of the six choose to nibble around the spoon. The other three decide to help it off the spoon and onto the plate—the preferred method, according to the Bergins.

The Soup Spoon Sundae adds a chapter (or at least a footnote) to the sundae saga. There is something quite heartening in this smaller-than-life perspective, and it's easy to see how some people, especially weight-conscious types, might order a Soup Spoon Sundae and feel wholly virtuous about it.

Chapter 26

DOWN THE DIXIE TRAIL

"You can't have everything.
Where would you put it?"

—STEVEN WRIGHT

*A*fter World War II, the "Dixie Trail," the new system of linked highways from New York to south Florida, was traveled by thousands of northerners seeking a warmer climate, inexpensive land and a friendly working or retirement environment. Florida soon grew into the South's most populous state.

In 1946, at the beginning of the boom, Jack Udell sold his coffee shop in Stamford, Connecticut, packed up most of his family and moved to Hollywood, Florida, where he opened a beachfront hotdog stand. Soon after, he was joined by his 18-year-old son, Monroe, who'd left a soda jerk position at Stamford's Nutmeg Fountain.

For 10 years, father and son worked side by side, but when a space in a newly-built strip mall in nearby Dania opened up, Monroe jumped at the opportunity to get into business for himself. "Since I was Jack's son, I named the place Jaxson's," recalls Monroe. "I added an 'X' to mark the spot."

On opening day, a single scoop of ice cream sold for 10 cents; a double was 15 cents, and a hot fudge sundae, 45 cents.

All ice creams, plus toppings and syrups, are still made on the premises. Jaxson's features as many as 50 different creamy creations at any given time, with several flavors unlike those usually found elsewhere, such as Tropical Coconut, Piña Colada and Bubblegum. Jaxson's sundae makers have always diligently topped their concoctions with generous allotments of freshly-whipped cream.

"We don't believe in portion control," explains Monroe, a maximalist. "Our oversized servings are *out of control.*"

Even with inflated sizes for everything on the menu, nothing comes close to The Kitchen Sink, served in a stainless-steel hotel pan supported on a wooden base with drain pipe attached.

A minimum of four customers pay $9.95 each to choose three flavors of ice cream for assembly in the "sink." Ice creams are flooded with chocolate syrup, cherry-pineapple topping, crushed strawberries and marshmallow créme, surrounded with split bananas, showered with whipped cream and sprinkled with nuts. Burning sparklers add pyrotechnics, as the wail of a fire-truck siren announces its delivery to the table.

A visit to Jaxson's is a celebration of the ice cream parlor experience, complete with a trove of early, nearly-forgotten fountain formulas and a colorful, feel-good setting, just oozing with nostalgia. Part of the fun of coming here is watching fellow sweet tooths tackle their enormous banana splits, colossal parfaits and over-the-top sundaes.

If only Jack could see his son now.

Monroe Udell, Jaxson's sole proprietor for half a century, has amassed a sterling record of achievement at what has become a South Florida landmark. In an era of constant change, it's comforting to know that some things, at least, seem to stay the same. One of those things is Jaxson's Ice Cream Parlor.

FOR KIDS OF ALL AGES

Walt Disney, the man who built an empire on themes of childhood innocence, was something of a kid himself, craving ice cream sundaes, and serving them up to friends at the full-scale soda fountain he had constructed in his home's basement. Today's Disney resorts haven't ignored their founder's passion: to wit, the Disney property in Vero Beach, Florida, and its Beaches & Cream Soda Shop. Get in line for sundaes like the "No Way Jose," a peanut butter and hot fudge-covered concoction with scoops of chocolate and vanilla ice cream, peanut butter and chocolate morsels, whipped cream and a cherry.

LIVING LEGEND

First in the hearts and stomachs of those who remember family-owned Jahn's Ice Cream Parlors in and around New York City, plus one in Florida, is the masterwork, called The Kitchen Sink, which, according to menus, featured "everything else but." The last open Jahn's (in the Richmond Hill section of the borough of Queens), although not run by Jahn's descendants, still offers this 17-scoop creation, now served in a punch bowl instead of a big pan.

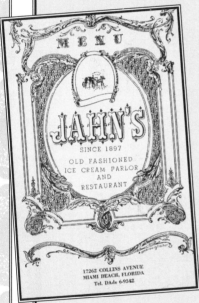

MENU

JAHN'S
SINCE 1897
OLD FASHIONED
ICE CREAM PARLOR
AND
RESTAURANT

17262 COLLINS AVENUE
MIAMI BEACH, FLORIDA
Tel. DAde 6-9342

MENU FROM THE NOW-GONE MIAMI OUTPOST OF JAHN'S.

OLD MENUS TOLD THE STORY OF HOW JAHN'S BEGAN:

"The year is 1888—winter—snowing to beat all ice cream. A sailing vessel makes port at New York and who steps off but John Jahn, age 14, hereafter called Papa. A real greenhorn with nothing but ambition. Five years of working at a bakery at ten dollars per month with board. Papa didn't go too much for the heat, having come from a cold country, so he left and got a job as an ice cream maker for a store in Brooklyn. He froze along and finally met Mama, at a dancing school called Weber's. A married man has to be able to support a family so Papa opened his first store in the Bronx at 138th Street and Alexander Avenue in 1897. More years of selling sodas at five cents and ice cream at twenty-five cents a quart, which was never measured but just tossed into whatever kind of can or dish you brought along."

THE RECIPES

SNOWBALL (FOR SNOWBIRDS)

Dip 3 large scoops of vanilla ice cream into a tall goblet and cover with marshmallow sauce. Sprinkle generously with shredded coconut, top with whipped cream, finish with a cherry.

JAXSON'S SURPRISE

Roll 3 large scoops of vanilla ice cream over chopped pecans until the surfaces are fully coated. Place scoops into a tall sundae glass and cover with hot fudge. Garnish with whipped cream, and place a maraschino cherry at the top.

–*Jaxson's*, Dania, Florida

Chapter 27

SOUTHERN COMFORT ZONE

*"In the South, we have a way
of expanding our relatedness to other people
through food."*

—ELLEN ROLFES, *THE SOUTHERN CULTURE COOKBOOK*

From Little Rock, I followed Highway 67 North for about 45 miles. I took Exit 42 onto Main Street, turned left at the White County Library, and on the next block a modest sign with red letters announced my arrival at the Yarnell Ice Cream Company, smack-dab in the middle of Searcy, Arkansas, where it was founded in 1932.

It was near the end of a particularly hot summer when an ambitious young man named Raymond Yarnell purchased a small, 10-year-old ice cream plant at this very spot. Those were the days before home freezers, when practically every town in Arkansas had its own ice cream plant. Yarnell's first trucks were cooled with ice and salt. Just like its ice cream freezers. Each morning, drivers had to chip ice by hand, then climb to the top of their trucks and dump it along with salt along the sides to keep the trucks cold.

"If you look closely at the truck in this picture, you'll notice the railing around the top," says Christina Yarnell, pointing to one of the photographs that line the walls of the company offices. "It kept the men from falling off while they loaded that ice and salt. On a long truck route, the men had to stop at ice houses in each town to add more ice and drain off the water."

Christina is the keeper of Yarnell's history. She is the fourth generation of the ice cream-making family, and its striking director of public relations. As a young girl, she listened to her grandfather, Albert, tell how he had made ice cream deliveries on his bicycle. Yarnell is run today by Christina's father, Rogers. "Family stories," Christina says, "are the bonds that keep families alive."

Because of family stories, Christina Yarnell can describe vividly days well before her time. "In those times, remember, people couldn't keep ice cream at home," she explains. "There was a special day of the year for ice cream—the Fourth of July. Our rural communities had no electricity, and country stores could not keep ice cream on hand. So the big Independence Day picnic was one of the few occasions in the year when folks could buy all the ice cream they could eat.

"Concession stands dotted the picnic grounds across the street from our plant, with ice cream packed in five-gallon tubs. Great-grandfather made just a few basic flavors, so local folks took to dressing up their dishes

FARM TO FOUNTAIN

*B*raum's is the only major ice cream maker and retailer in the United States that milks its own cows. Back in the Depression, Henry Braum was a Kansas dairy farmer with a small milk and butter processing plant. By 1940, he'd added ice cream-making to use up his milk surplus. After college, Henry's son, Bill, joined his dad in business and began to open retail ice cream stores.

In 1968, Bill Braum sold his 61 Peter Pan stores, and moved lock, stock and barrel to Tuttle, Oklahoma. Today, the Braum dairy cows number 10,000 and graze on 40,000 acres. And Braum's Ice Cream operates 280 retail stores in Oklahoma, Texas, Kansas, Missouri and Arkansas.

COURTESY OF BRAUM'S

Braum cows produce the milk that's made into Braum's ice cream, delivered in a Braum truck to a Braum's store, where you can enjoy a Braum's Strawberry Shortcake Sundae. Holy cow!

CAJUN
COURAGE

*F*olks from all over America have made the pilgrimage to Robin's in Henderson, Louisiana, 30 miles from Baton Rouge. They come for chef Lionel Robin's unpretentious Cajun specialties, perfected over three decades of restaurant cooking.

Robin's Hot Chocolate Sundae is not for faint hearts; its basis is Tabasco ice cream. The chef makes the ice cream with a standard vanilla recipe, to which he adds one ounce of pepper sauce for every quart of heavy cream. If you want to make this at home, he says, it's important to shake the bottle of Tabasco vigorously before releasing the sauce.

"After the first two or three bites" [of the ice cream], Robin says, "you begin to get the flavor of the Tabasco, which doesn't get any more hot."

To make the sundae, he pours chocolate syrup over the Tabasco ice cream. "Chocolate and Tabasco go well together," he insists.

of ice cream with honey, molasses and home-made preserves, sundae-style."

The little ice cream company began to grow at the end of the 1930s when Yarnell purchased its first electrically refrigerated truck. It held 650 gallons, and Ray's wife, Hallie, worried about whether their company would ever be able to sell so much ice cream.

Over the years, most of the community ice cream companies of Arkansas disappeared. Yarnell now not only dominates the ice cream market in its home state, but has grown to become a competitor from Texas to Mississippi. It employs 225 people.

Milk and cream for Yarnell's ice creams are delivered fresh from the dairy farmers' cooperative in northwest Arkansas three times a day, and tested for quality immediately upon arrival. The liquids are pumped into a holding tank, pasteurized, homogenized, then aged overnight. Following the addition of sugar with a high-speed blender, the mix is drawn into a flavor vat where fruit purees or colors are added. Next, the mix enters a "barrel" freezer where it is frozen as rotating dashers incorporate air. The result properly can be called ice cream.

Fruits, nuts, candy, cookies or other ingredients are added to the semi-frozen slurry, which has a consistency similar to soft-serve ice cream. Cartons travel down a conveyor system and slide onto a carousel where they are filled, capped, boxed and shrink-wrapped by machine, before being whisked into the hardening room for blast freezing—the colder the temperature, the faster the hardening, the smoother the product. Finished products are stacked by flavor, sorted by orders, and loaded into Yarnell's fleet of refrigerated trucks, ready for delivery.

After I saw more ice cream than most people see in a lifetime, Christina suggested a place where I could put Yarnell's ice cream to the sundae test. We drove a few blocks to a coffee house/restaurant called the Midnight Oil, next door to U-Haul. The bicycle parked outside belonged to Midnight Oil owner, Matthew West.

The interior presented a comfy setting with a dozen tables and 40 or so chairs set on a hardwood floor, plus a large couch and overstuffed easy chairs around a fireplace. I'm told that Midnight Oil (yes, it's open that late) is popular with students from nearby Harding College; it also draws morning coffee and lunch-break regulars in the *Leave-it-to-Beaver* town of Searcy.

Matthew chatted with us. "We're in a dry county," he explained, "so folks in these parts stop by for a sundae the way people in other places visit a bar." He says he selected "Homemade Vanilla" for his establishment after trying all four Yarnell vanillas. "It's right in between the Angel Food Vanilla and not quite to French Vanilla," says West. "The creaminess holds up in sundaes and shakes."

So what about that sundae? The Midnight Oil's Chocolate Sundae arrived as plain as could be. A classic tulip held two scoops of the fresh, white ice cream, covered with Hershey's dark brown chocolate syrup, decorated with a mound of whipped cream (no cherry).

As I dug in with my tall spoon, before I even tasted the sundae, I knew I'd like it. Visiting a town like Searcy, seeing ice cream made, and finally sitting down to a sundae was an emotional shortcut back to childhood comfort.

THE RECIPE

FROZEN MUG SUNDAE

*D*ip 2 large scoops of vanilla ice cream into a frosted beer mug, and cover with choice of toppings (hot fudge sauce, caramel sauce, chocolate sauce, crushed strawberries, blueberry syrup or sorghum molasses). Garnish with whipped cream, sprinkle with roasted almonds and place a maraschino cherry at the top.

-Cracker Barrel Restaurants, 485 locations in 41 states

Chapter 28

SUNDAE KIND OF LOVE

"I just had two double fudge sundaes."

–KRAMER (MICHAEL RICHARDS) IN *SEINFELD*

For Kramer, hot fudge substituted for love. Others find it goes with romance. Author Teresa Lust described the connection between food and desire as "the luxurious feel on the tongue of melting ice cream—there is no denying that some foods have the power to arouse the senses."

In *Much Depends on Dinner*, Margaret Visser points out that ice cream long has been seen as "female" in northern cultures.

The scoop of ice cream in a sundae dish rests on a ragged edge called the "skirt." Soda jerks have been taught to provide a neat skirt around each dip.

Couples therapist Pauline Falstrom explains what a hot fudge sundae and amour have in common. If you gulp down a sundae so rapidly that you hardly take time to enjoy it, you likely have a similar problem in your love life, she suggests.

Falstrom recommends eating your sundae very slowly. Taste the coldness of the vanilla ice cream and notice how it feels in contrast to the

---

GOING THROUGH THE MOTIONS

Academy Award-winning actress Loretta Young once revealed how she maintained a rapturous expression on her face during countless takes. She confessed that whenever she was in the arms of a dashing, leading man, she pretended she was face to face with a hot fudge sundae.

hot fudge. Contemplate the iced goblet and the long-handled silver spoon. Savor the placement of the ground walnuts on real whipped cream, explore their crunchy texture, then examine the contrast between the nuts and the softness of the cream. Save the plump red cherry for last.

Connections between sundaes and sensuality are not new. Frederic Prokosch, in *Voices: A Memoir*, describes an evening in Paris in 1922: "That night for dessert we had a Singapore Ice Cream, which was studded with ginger and covered with whipped cream. Gertrude Stein looked very voluptuous as she licked at her spoon, which she did with half-closed eyes and a slow, stately rhythm. Her tongue suggested the bow of an expert fiddler who is playing a languid and delicious adagio."

In *Brighton Beach Memoirs*, one of Neil Simon's characters explains, "It's amazing how quickly you recover from misery when someone offers you ice cream."

HOW TO THROW A SUNDAE PARTY

Liks (née Lickety Split in 1976) throws lots of Denver's best sundae parties. Many enjoy Liks' sundaes in its splendid shop, but owner Jay Thompson reports that catered ice cream bashes at private parties, charity dos or company picnics are one way to beat the long lines outside his institution.

For groups of 30 or more, Thompson's crew pre-dips any three ice creams (from a list of 250 flavors, believe it or not!) and ladles up any three toppings (from a not quite so long list of favorites), then packs it all up with whipped cream, cherries, and plenty of dry ice to keep everything cold and delivers it to as far away as Boulder. The tab is a modest $2.85 per person.

"Six hundred people attended our biggest sundae party," boasts Thompson. "Our most unusual affair was a fabulously indulgent pool party in downtown Denver—the adults got very creative with the whipped cream and cherries."

Gael Greene has compared great food to love: "The more you have the more you want." In *Bite*, she rhapsodizes over sundaes: "I sing of the do-it-yourself sundae freak-out with a discriminating hoard of haute toppings—wet walnuts, hot fudge, home-

made peach conserve . . . inspiring a madness that lifts masks, shatters false dignity and bridges all generation gaps."

THE RECIPES

SINFUL CHOCOLATE SUNDAE

Dip 2 large scoops of double-chocolate ice cream into a tall sundae goblet. Cover once with marshmallow syrup, cover again with hot fudge sauce. Insert 2 Heath Bars into either side of the ice cream, garnish with whipped cream and place a Hershey's Kiss at the top.

–Mad Martha's, Vineyard Haven, Massachusetts

Chapter 29

COUNTER CULTURE

*"Happily, there is not a wrong way
to build an ice cream sundae."*

–CHARITY FERREIRA

This conclusion of a noted pastry chef is shared by almost everyone in the dessert business. Still, after the better part of a century, you would think there were no sundae rules left to break. Yet just a few decades ago, Steve Herrell's "mix-in," the blended-by-hand combination of ice cream and sundae toppings, launched a new craze in the ice cream industry.

Herrell grew up in Washington D.C., then ambled off to Boston. After a brief stint teaching, the young wanderer spent three years driving a cab in and around Boston, where he daydreamed about things like the ice creams he'd churned at home as a kid and about going into business for himself. Then one day he spotted an empty storefront in suburban Somerville. Ice cream history would soon be made.

On June 29, 1973, the opening of Steve's Ice Cream introduced Boston to premium, low-overrun ice cream, a break from the air-filled factory products. Besides exotic flavors, Steve Herrell turned his personal passion for Heath Bars into a new ice cream feature.

He wanted to batch-blend the companionable milk chocolate or the English-style toffee flavor Heath into his ice cream, but he couldn't decide which flavor to use. So he left the decision to customer preference. Both types of candy bar were cut up into small pieces, a customer picked one and Steve or another staffer used a hand-held fountain spade to blend the selected candy into the customer's chosen ice cream flavor.

It was an easy leap from Heath bars to Reese's Peanut Butter Cups and broken Oreo cookies, closely followed by Nestle's Crunch, Snickers, Kit Kats and M&Ms. Ingredients were folded into servings right before customers' eyes, providing not only individualized concoctions but visual entertainment to boot. "By the nature of it," admits Herrell, "it's a performance."

In 1980, Steve sold out to investors who then opened more shops and placed premixed ice creams in supermarkets. When their business foundered, Herrell decided to make a comeback--not as "Steve's," but as "Herrell's."

Steve Herrell still rules the roost at locations in and around Boston. Meanwhile, around the country his custom mix-ins have inspired glorious copyists.

After working at Steve's during her college days in Boston, Amy Miller opened her own ice cream shop back home in Austin, Texas, in 1986, blending ingredients under the parlance of "crush-ins."

"Most ice cream dishes are served too cold and they freeze taste buds," says Amy, whose servers learn to soften the ice cream, as her mentor did, while blending in nuts, cookies, candy and fruit.

As Ms. Miller expanded into Houston and San Antonio, her success was noticed by Texas entrepreneurs Donald and Susan Sutherland. The Sutherlands--no relation to the acting family--developed their own ice cream emporiums, embracing the personalization of ice cream dishes and cones with the applied art of the confectionery mix-in. Beginning with a single store in Tempe, Arizona, in 1988, Cold Stone Creamery is the recognized leader in the mix-in category with over 1,000 units in 47 states.

"We'll never hesitate to acknowledge Steve Herrell as the grandfather of the concept," says Kevin Donnellan, the company's director of public

SWEET INSPIRATION

Ben Cohen and Jerry Greenfield credit Steve Herrell for providing advice and encouragement. The two men journeyed to "Mecca" (the original Steve's) before they opened the first Ben and Jerry's in a renovated gas station in Burlington, Vermont. They not only made super-rich-style ice creams like those mixed at Steve's, they spent years modifying equipment and production techniques so they could put all those "mix-in" ingredients inside their ice creams at the factory. The duo had become famous for both their flavors and their ecological hopes by the time they sold their booming business to Unilever in 2000.

relations, "but we believe we've taken the mix-in to the next level with our frozen granite stone."

The centerpiece of Cold Stone Creamery stores is the "frost top" made of black granite, a material chosen for low porosity and moisture absorption, superior strength, and excellent thermal conduction. Installed on the counter over an Italian gelato-style cooler, the stone provides a constant 16-degree working surface throughout each mix-in procedure.

The company employs over 25,000 servers; each hire must survive an audition-like interview. Prospective crew members are asked to "bust a move," that is, to perform a song or dance that shows off his or her personality. Prospects are also split into groups to develop a collaborative skit, a test of teamwork. Job applicants are not strictly assessed on their singing or dancing ability, according to Donnellan, who says energy and enthusiasm count for a great deal. Cold Stone's performing servers put the scream back into ice cream as they mish, mash, muddle and mingle.

I suppose the popularity of the mix-in can be attributed to Americans' love for absolute freedom and their constant need for the newer and better. Nothing is more liberating than inventing your own personal combination of gooey, chunky, sweet and crunchy.

THE RECIPES

QUADRUPLE CHOCOLATE SUNDAE

*D*ip 2 large scoops of chocolate ice cream into a large sundae goblet. Cover with hot fudge, garnish with chocolate whipped cream (recipe below), and sprinkle chocolate chips over the top.

CHOCOLATE WHIPPED CREAM

1 cup heavy cream
2 tablespoons confectioners' sugar
1/2 teaspoon pure vanilla extract

*1/4 cup unsweetened Dutch-
process cocoa powder*

In a mixing bowl, whip the cream until the cream is slightly thickened. Add the remaining ingredients and continue whipping until the cream holds its shape. Spoon on top of the sundae. Makes 2 cups.

-*Herrell's*, Boston, Massachusetts

COLD STONE ORIGINALS

"Insist upon yourself," wrote Ralph Waldo Emerson. "Be original." With over a dozen kinds of ice cream and three dozen mix-in ingredients to choose from at Cold Stone Creamery stores, it's a good bet that most of us can come up with an unprecedented culinary masterpiece. But, for the less inventive, each store provides a menu of formulas called "Originals."

Blend strawberries, roasted almonds, and fudge into banana ice cream for a *Banana Split Decision*; combine chocolate chips, brownie bits, fudge and chocolate ice cream to achieve *Chocolate Devotion*; lump together roasted almonds, caramel, and pieces of Heath bar into coffee ice cream, and the concoction is called *Coffee Lovers Only*.

Chapter 30

BACK TO THE FUTURE

"I believe the future is only the past again, entered through another gate."

—ARTHUR WING PINERO

Something about the ice cream sundae-and I believe that something has to do with innocently delicious childhood memories--lends itself to sweet nostalgia. Many of the foods we crave in the 21st century seem to reprise kinder, gentler moments in our lives. Sensing the reassurance many customers crave, especially at dessert time, some influential restaurateurs meet us exactly where we want to be.

Consider Sheldon Fireman. By almost any measure, he is a clever entrepreneur. Mind you, he is not a groundbreaker. Rather, he mixes and matches familiar conventions and, in the process, he has created a half dozen popular restaurants in Manhattan. He is an expert at making old themes new again.

As a youth, Shelly worked at Krum's ice cream parlor, across from Loew's Paradise movie theater, on the Grand Concourse in the Bronx. "We loaded the truck with ice cream according to the ethnicity of the neighborhood," he recalls. "If it was a Jewish section, the delivery was mostly chocolate; in the Irish sections, vanilla; the Italian neighborhood's favorite flavor was coffee. The job paid 35 cents an hour, and I wasn't allowed to accept tips."

At age 14, he was promoted to Saturday soda jerk. "Krum's was the largest confectionery in the Bronx, with maybe two hundred stools at the counter," he recalls. "They were famous for ice cream sundaes, and I made more of them than I could ever count."

Today, the cash registers at Manhattan restaurants tell him that even jaded New Yorkers crave comfort food. "There are only two questions to ask about food," maintains Fireman. "Is it good and is it authentic? People are open to new ideas, but not if it means disturbing our food history. Our customers want reassuring dishes—food designed less to impress than simply to enjoy."

CREATE THE FUTURE

In Toronto, there's one sundae maker who produces remarkable sundaes from ice creams he makes himself. Gary Stephen Theodore's motto is: "Learn the past, watch the present, and create the future." He has been upstaging many of his counterparts to the south ever since he opened the first Caffé Demetré in 1989, and he continues to raise the bar for ice cream retailers everywhere.

Theodore traces his roots to a Greek-immigrant ancestor who operated the Yorkville Candy Kitchen in York, South Carolina, back in the early 1900s. Three generations later, Theodore is making ice creams whose richness and flavor might have impressed his great grandfather even if their names were unfamiliar. Theodore's high-concept ice cream parlors now number a dozen locations in and around Toronto.

"Ice cream is the easiest food to glamorize," says Theodore, who supplemented family traditions by attending Penn State's prestigious Ice Cream Science program. His passionate approach for Caffé Demetré has produced sundaes on top of French toast, sundaes on top of Belgian waffles and sundaes inside French crepes. Among the masterpieces on his wildly creative menu is the Freudian Dip: One scoop of Chocolatta, a rich chocolate ice cream, rolled in white chocolate chunks, and one scoop of Belgian white chocolate ice cream rolled in dark chocolate chunks, served on a bed of triple fudge sauce topped with more triple fudge.

At Shelly's New York (in the same storefront that once housed a Horn & Hardart Automat), the most spectacular sundae is called Mama's Mixing Bowl a family-size wooden bowl of warm chocolate ganache (equal parts of melted chocolate and cream) and chocolate cookie crumbles, topped with chocolate ice cream, served with a wooden spoon filled with whipped cream, for mixing in. This dessert, like some of Manhattan's

ONLY AN HONEST SUNDAE IS WORTH EATING ANY DAY OF THE WEEK.

architectural wonders, can be looked at with pleasure from any angle.

As you learn more about food, you expand the way you think about it, and Fireman's knowledge manifests itself in his restaurants. His dishes are deeply influenced by traditional recipes and standard techniques, and that's why he believes customers are so enamored of his places. "I want you to eat food you have an urge for, food that's in your memory bank," he says. "I want my places to be loved. I need you to come back and come back often, so I offer familiarity on the menu."

Fireman, a true believer in the ice cream sundae, has been toying with it and derivative desserts since his days behind the soda fountain. With successive ventures, his vision became grander. "They've never really gone out of fashion at all," he insists, "and they never will. The sundae stands the test of time, even in our famously fickle industry. Everyone loves the ice cream sundae."

A PREDICTION THAT HASN'T COME TRUE: SUNDAES IN PILL FORM

🍒

"*He remained obstinately gloomy the whole afternoon; wouldn't talk to Lenina's friends (of whom they met dozens in the ice-cream soda bar between the wrestling bouts); and in spite of his misery absolutely refused to take the half-gramme Raspberry Sundae which she pressed upon him. 'I'd rather be myself,' he said. 'Myself and nasty. Not somebody else, however jolly.'*"

—Aldous Huxley, *Brave New World*

THE RECIPES

HOT FUDGE SUNDAE

This classic, served in Brooklyn Diner (another Fireman establishment) attracts the likes of Sarah Jessica Parker to sundae in the city. New York Magazine called it the "Best Hot Fudge Sundae in New York."

LADLE 2 OUNCES OF HOT FUDGE SAUCE INTO THE BOTTOM OF A TALL SUNDAE GLASS. DIP ONE LARGE SCOOP OF VANILLA ICE CREAM INTO THE GLASS, AND ADD 3 OUNCES OF HOT FUDGE SAUCE. DIP ANOTHER 2 LARGE SCOOPS OF VANILLA ICE CREAM AND ADD ANOTHER 3 OUNCES OF HOT FUDGE SAUCE. DIP ONE MORE LARGE SCOOP OF VANILLA ICE CREAM AND COVER WITH A HEAPING TABLESPOON OF WET WALNUTS. GARNISH WITH WHIPPED CREAM AND PLACE A STEMMED MARASCHINO CHERRY AT THE TOP.

–Brooklyn Diner USA, New York, New York

CHOCOLATE JALAPENO SUNDAE

Here is the trend-setting dessert popularized at the Tucson restaurant of Janos Wilder, a James Beard Award winner. Tiny snips of jalapeno are added to a vanilla ice cream recipe to make this sundae base. The principle is the same as adding, say, chocolate chips, but you might want to use pepper bits more sparingly. Wilder's sundae reflects the Mexican tradition of combining spicy and sweet, hot and cold.

PLACE ONE LAYER OF WHITE CHOCOLATE GANACHE (EQUAL PARTS OF MELTED WHITE CHOCOLATE AND CREAM) INTO A TALL, PRE-CHILLED SUNDAE GOBLET, THEN ADD 3 LARGE SCOOPS OF JALAPENO-VANILLA ICE CREAM. SPRINKLE WITH SUGARED PECANS AND COVER WITH HOT FUDGE SAUCE. GARNISH WITH WHIPPED CREAM AND PLACE A SPICY, CHILI-SHAPED COOKIE AT THE TOP.

–Janos, Tucson, Arizona

Chapter 31

SUNDAE HALL OF FAME

*"All that really matters is that the people
you love are happy and healthy.
Everything else is just sprinkles
on the sundae."*

–PAUL WALKER

Sundaes shine like bright stars in the ice cream parlors of America. However, unlike celestial bodies dotting the night skies, these stars acquire their glow from dedicated ice cream artisans behind the nation's soda fountains. Their special magic makes every day a sundae.

Since most of these folks consider it impolite to toot their own horns, I am delighted to toot it for them. Through my website at www.ice-creamsundae.com, I receive hundreds of recommendations for establishments where the humble practice of sundae-making has been elevated to the status of art. While I haven't personally visited every place mentioned, I depend on a network of ice-cream-industry professionals to help me screen sundae-serving establishments.

Here, then, is the cream of the crop: over 500 destinations, scattered throughout our 50 states, that deserve special recognition for the versatility, construction technique and respect for tradition with which their sundaes are executed. These are the sundae stars in the firmament of American culture.

Alabama

FOLEY
Lower Alabama Mud
Stacey Rexall Drugs
121 W. Laurel Ave.
(251) 943-7191

MOBILE
Red, White & Blue Sundae
Old Dutch Ice Cream
Shoppe
2511 Old Shell Road
(251) 544-1077

TUSCALOOSA
Tuscaloosa Turtle
Papa's College Custard
1383 McFarland Blvd. E.
(205) 247-2690

TUSCUMBIA
*Alabama Slammer
Sundae*
Palace Drug Store
100 S. Main St.
(256) 386-8210

SEARCY
Black and White Sundae
Midnight Oil
801 E. Race Ave.
(501) 268-9014

Alaska

CORDOVA
Sundae-of-the-Day
Northern Delights
501 First Street
(907) 424-4328

FAIRBANKS
Wild Blueberry Sundae
Hot Licks Homemade Ice
Cream
3453 College Road
(907) 479-7813

SEWARD
Black Raspberry Sundae
Harbor Street Creamery
307 S. Harbor Street
(907) 224-8818

Arizona

GILBERT
Bananas Foster Sundae
Streamers Ice Cream

Parlor
1166 S. Gilbert Road
(480) 635-9222

PHOENIX
Gooey Nuts Sundae
MacAlpine's Soda
Fountain
2303 N. 7th St.
(602) 262-5545

Suicide Sundae
Mary Coyle Ice Cream
Parlor
5521 N. Seventh Ave.
(602) 265-6266

SCOTTSDALE
Top Hat Sundae
Sugar Bowl Ice Cream
Parlor
4005 N. Scottsdale Rd.
(480) 946-0051

TUSCON
Austin Delight
Austin's No. 1 Ice Cream
2920 E. Broadway Blvd.
(520) 327-3892

Arkansas

BENTON
Black and White Sundae
Jerry Van Dyke's Soda
Shoppe
107 S. Market St.
(501) 860-5500

EUREKA SPRINGS
*Strawberry Shortcake
Sundae*
Village Ice Cream Parlor
308 Village Circle
(479) 253-5131

HARDY
Hot Caramel Sundae
Hardy Malt Shoppe
124 Main St.
(870) 856-6258

IMBODEN
Pineapple Sundae
Joy's Drive-In
1037 W. 3rd St.
(870) 869-2524

LITTLE ROCK
Banana Split

Asher Dairy Bar
7105 Colonel Glenn Rd.
(501) 562-1085

*Cashew Caramel Coffee
Sundae*
The Purple Cow
8026 Cantrell Road
(501) 221-3555

Chocolate Shortcake
Dixie Café
1301 Rebsamen Park Rd.
(501) 663-9336

MALVERN
Butterscotch Sundae
Mel's Dairy Bar
1228 Stanley St.
(501) 337-0696

NORTH LITTLE ROCK
Chocolate Sundae
Dairyland Drive-In
2306 Highway 161
(501) 945-4593

ROGERS
The Original Straw-ana
Andy's Frozen Custard
2205 W. Walnut
(479) 636-2639

SEARCY
Black and White Sundae
Midnight Oil
801 E. Race Ave.
(501) 268-9014

California

ALAMEDA
Granddaddy Sundae
Tucker's Ice Cream
1349 Park St.
(510) 522-4960

ALHAMBRA
Banana Split
Fosselman's
1824 W. Main St.
(626) 282-6533

Waffle Works Sundae
Twohey's
1224 N. Atlantic Blvd.
(626) 284-7387

ARROYO GRANDE
Freight Car Sundae
Doc Burnstein's Ice
Cream Lab
114 W. Branch St.
(805) 474-4068

CASTRO VALLEY
Berry Go Round
Knudsen's Ice Creamery
3323 Castro Valley Blvd.
(510) 582-2775

CHESTER
Mt. Lassen Sundae
Lassen Drug Co.
220 Main St.
(530) 258-2222

CHICO
Boysenberry Sundae
Shubert's Ice Cream &
Candy
178 E. Seventh St.
(530) 342-7163

HANFORD
Superior Special
Superior Dairy
325 N. Douty St.
(559) 582-0481

JULIAN
Rosemarie Sundae
Julian Drug Store & Soda
Fountain
2134 Main St.
(760) 765-0332

LOS ANGELES
Mickey's Masterpiece
Disney's Soda Fountain &
Studio Store
6834 Hollywood Blvd.
(818) 845-3110

MANHATTAN BEACH
Surfside Sundae
Manhattan Beach
Creamery
1120 Manhattan Ave.
(310) 372-1155

MAMMOUTH LAKES
Papa Bear Banana Split
Mammoth Lakes Ice
Creamery
3704 Main
(760) 924-5994

MODESTO
Perfect Sundae
Ice Cream Company
2401 E. Orangeburg Ave.
(209) 578-3112

OAKLAND
Black and Tan Sundae
Dreyer's Ice Cream Shop
5925 College Avenue
(510) 654-6799

Banana Special
Fenton's Creamery
4226 Piedmont Ave.
(510) 658-7000

OCEANSIDE
Hot Caramel Sundae
Nana's & Pop Pops Sweet
Shop
280 Harbor Dr. S.
(760) 722-1723

ORANGE
Oreo Brownie Sundae
Watson Soda Fountain &
Lunch Counter
116 E. Chapman Ave.
(714) 633-1050

PALO ALTO
Banana Boat
Rick's Rather Rich Ice
Cream
3946 Middlefield Rd.
(650) 493-6553

PASADENA
Fair Oaks Sundae
Fair Oaks Pharmacy and
Soda Fountain
1526 Mission St.
(626) 799-1414

Rose Bowl Banana Royale
Soda Jerks
219 S. Fair Oaks
(626) 583-8031

SACRAMENTO
Banana Berry Sundae
Gunther's Quality Ice
Cream
2801 Franklin Blvd.
(916) 457-6646

Black and Tan Sundae
Leatherby's Family
Creamery

2333 Arden Way
(916) 920-8382

ST. HELENA
Banana Split
Big Dipper
1336A Oak Ave.
(707) 963-2616

SAN DIEGO
Strawberry Sundae
Oasis Ice Cream Parlor
1832 Coronado Ave.
(619) 429-8980

SAN FRANCISCO
Strike It Rich
Ghirardelli Chocolate
Manufactory & Soda
Fountain
900 North Point St.
(415) 474-1414

Waffle Cone Sundae
Joe's Ice Cream
5351 Geary Blvd. 18th Ave.
(415) 751-1950

La Tropica
Maggie Mudd Ice Cream
Parlor
903 Cortland
(415) 641-5291

Love's Delight
St. Francis Fountain
2801 24th St.
(415) 826-4200

Gold Rush Sundae
Swensen's Ice Cream
1999 Hyde St.
(415) 775-6818

SAN JOSE
Belly Buster
Sweet Retreat Ice Cream
Parlor
6061 Cahalan Ave.
(408) 629-8139

SANTA ANA
Pig Out
Hans' Homemade Ice
Cream
3640 S. Bristol St.
(714) 979-8815

SANTA CRUZ
Epicenter Sundae
Marianne's Ice Cream
1020 Ocean St.
(831) 458-1447

SEBASTAPOL
The Screamin' Mimi
Screamin' Mimi's
6902 Sebastopol Ave.
(707) 823-5902

SUTTER CREEK
Volcano
Sutter Ice Cream
Emporium
51 Main St.
(209) 267-0543

WOODSIDE
Buck's Ice Cream Sundae
Buck's of Woodside
3062 Woodside Rd.
(650) 851-8010

Colorado

BOULDER
Pineapple Sundae
Boulder Ice Cream
Shoppe
637 G. South Broadway
(303) 494-2002

BRECKENRIDGE
Strawberry Sundae
Greta's Ice Cream
114 S. Main
(970) 453-7275

COLORADO SPRINGS
Believe It or Not
Michelle's
122 North Tejon St.
(719) 633-5089

Hot Fudge Sundae
Josh & John's Naturally
Homemade Ice Creams
111 E. Pike's Peak Ave.
(719) 632-0299

DENVER
Caramel Cashew Sundae
Daily Scoop
3506 E. 12th Ave.
(303) 388-3245

Ice Cream Sundae Party
Liks
2039 13th Avenue
(303) 321-2370

ESTES PARK
Matterhorn Sundae
The Malt Shop
125 Moraine Ave.
(970) 586-3542

FAIRPLAY
Peanut Butter Sundae
Silver Scoop Creamery
456 Front St.
(719) 836-3403

FORT COLLINS
Saturdae
Walrus Ice Cream
Company
125 W. Mountain Ave.
(970) 482-5919

GRAND JUNCTION
Hot Fudge Sundae
Pappy's Ice Cream Parlor
560 Main St.
(970) 241-9565

LITTLETON
Chocolate Sundae
Red Rooster Creamery
4004 Red Cedar Dr.
(303) 791-9735

LOVELAND
Dirt and Worms Sundae
Penguins Ice Cream Shop
1171 Eagle Dr.
(970) 461-5924

LYONS
S'More Sundae
Lyons Soda Fountain
400 Main St.
(303) 823-5393

SEDALIA
Raspberry Sundae
Rock Top Ice Cream Shop
5457 Manhart St.
(303) 660-5650

Connecticut

BETHEL
Black Cherry Sundae
Dr. Mike's Ice Cream Shop
158 Greenwood Ave.
(203) 792-4388

BRIDGEPORT
Brownie Sundae
Timothy's
2974 Fairfield Ave.
(203) 366-7496

BRISTOL
Maple Walnut Sundae
Dunphy's Ice Cream
Parlor
912 Stafford Ave.
(860) 584-8558

DERBY
A Sundae to Remember
Sundaes by the River
418 Roosevelt Dr.
(203) 736-9238

EAST HADDAM
Sundae Shake
Jennifer's Ice Cream
388 Main St.
(203) 468-1573

GUILFORD
Downside Watson
Ashley's Ice Cream Café
942 Boston Post Rd.
(203) 458-3040

HARTFORD
Peanut Butter Sundae
Roxie's Gulf Coast
Kitchen
341 Franklin Ave.
(860) 296-0087

KENT
Dippidopolus
Stosh's Ice Cream
38 N. Main St.
(860) 927-4495

MIDDLEBURY
Hot Butterscotch Sundae
Johnny's Dairy Bar
512 Middlebury Rd.
(203) 758-2623

MILFORD
*Upside Down Banana
Split*
Sundae House
499 New Haven Ave.
(203) 878-0143

MOOSUP
L.L. Sundae
Ra Ra's Ice Cream Parlor
69 Prospect St.
(860) 564-3930

MYSTIC
Caramel Lover's Sundae
Mystic Drawbridge Ice
Cream
2 W. Main St.
(860) 572-7978

NEWINGTON
Wheelbarrow Sundae
Mortensen's
3145 Berlin Turnpike
(860) 666-8219

ORANGE
Sundae in a Shake
Dip Top
263 Boston Post Rd.
(203) 795-0664

PROSPECT
Galaxy Sundae
Big Dipper
91 Waterbury Rd.
(203) 758-3200

RIDGEFIELD
Hot Fudge Sundae
Mr. Shane's Homemade
Parlor
409 Main St.
(203) 431-8020

Peanut Butter Sundae
Ridgefield Ice Cream
Shop
680 Danbury Rd.
(203) 438-3094

STAMFORD
Gofer Pie
Gofer Ice Cream
869 High Ridge Road
(203) 504-3105

STORRS
Hot Fudge Sundae
UConn Dairy Bar

3636 Horsebarn Rd. Ext.
(860) 486-2634

THOMASTON
Fruit Cocktail Sundae
Jillie's Ice Cream Parlor
52 Main St.
(860) 283-8962

WEST HARTFORD
*Banana Nut Supreme
Sundae*
A.C. Petersen Farms
240 Park Rd.
(860) 233-8483

Delaware

DELAWARE CITY
Peach Sundae
Ice Cream Parlor
32 Clinton St.
(302) 836-9252

DOVER
Peanut Butter Cluster
Vitale's Homemade Ice
Cream
75 Greentree Dr.
(302) 674-8851

MILTON
*Marshmallow-Strawberry
Sundae*
King's Homemade Ice
Cream
302 Union St.
(302) 684-8900

NEW CASTLE
Peaches & Cream Sundae
Dairy Palace
2 Jay Drive
(302) 328-9740

REHOBOTH BEACH
C.M.P.
Mack's Ice Cream Parlor
3727 Highway One
(302) 227-1962

WILMINGTON
Humdinger
Molly's Old Fashioned Ice
Cream
900 Pettinaro Park Dr.
(302) 984-2773

District of Columbia

*Disfunctional Family
Sundae*
Afterwards Café (at
Kramerbooks)
1517 Connecticut Ave.,
NW
(202) 387-1462

Buttercup Sundae
Eddy's Ice Cream
2001 L St., NW
(202) 296-4818

Wet Walnut Sundae
Ice Cream Station
3528 12th St., NE
(202) 526-7419

Brownie Sundae
Max's Best
2416 Wisconsin Ave., NW
(202) 333-3111

Hot Caramel Sundae
Thomas Sweet
3214 P St., NW
(202) 337-0616

Florida

COCOA BEACH
Red & White
Ricky's Ice Cream Parlor
& Arcade
401 Meade Ave.
(321) 783-7549

DANIA
Snowball Sundae
Jaxson's
128 South Federal Hwy
(954) 923-4445

DELRAY BEACH
Hot Fudge Sundae
Foxy's
12 S.E. Fifth Ave.
(561) 276-9379

HOLLYWOOD
Hot Butterscotch Sundae
Siciliano's Frozen Custard
5917 Hollywood Blvd.
(954) 985-8050

KEY WEST
Rag Top Day Sundae
Jimmy Buffet's
Margaritaville
424A Fleming St.
(305) 296-9089

LAKE WALES
*Toll House Chocolate
Chip Sundae*
Garfield's
823 Eagle Ridge Dr.
(863) 678-9826

MIAMI
Deco Banana Split
11th Street Diner
1065 Washington Ave.
(305) 534-6373

The Frieze
Frieze Ice Cream Factory
1626 Michigan Ave.
(305) 538-0207

Peanut Butter Passion
Whip 'N Dip Ice Cream
1407 Sunset Dr.
(305) 665-2565

ORLANDO
Oinker
McDonald's European
Café
7344 Sand Lake Rd.
(407) 264-0770

ST. PETERSBURG
*German Chocolate
Tourist*
It's Custard, Mon
3739 49th St. N.
(727) 520-8608

TAMPA
Banana Split
Bo's Ice Cream
7101 N. Florida Ave.
(813) 234-3870

*Coconut Almond Joy
Sundae*
Tanya's & Matt's Ice
Creamiest
15742 N. Dale Mabry Hwy.
(813) 963-2766

VERO BEACH
Kitchen Sink Sundae

Beaches & Cream Soda
Shop
9250 Island Grove
Terrace
(772) 234-2000

Georgia

ATLANTA
Hot Fudge Sundae
Jake's Ice Cream
676 Highland Ave.
(404) 586-9972

DECATUR
*Sweet Georgia Brown
Sundae*
Crescent Moon Eatery
174 W. Ponce de Leon
(404) 377-5623

FAYETTEVILLE
*Hot Fudge Brownie
Sundae*
Scoops American Grille &
Creamery
1415 Hwy. 85 N.
(770) 461-8500

ROSWELL
Brownie Mae Sundae
Calico Cow Creamery and
Café
4401 Shallowford Rd.
(678) 205-3647

SAVANNAH
Banana Split
Leopold's Ice Cream
212 E. Broughton St.
(912) 234-4442

Hawaii

AIEA-OAHU
Clown Sundae
Ronnie's Ice Cream Parlor
& Restaurant
Westridge Center
98-150 Kaonohi St.
(808) 485-0995

HONOLULU
Hula Pie
Lappert's Ice Cream &
Coffee
3077 Koapaka St.
(808) 834-7623

Banana Royale
Zippy's
1210 Dillingham Blvd.
(808) 832-1750

PEARL CITY
Butterscotch Sundae
Dave's Hawaiian Ice
Cream
96-1361 Waihona St.
(808) 453-0500

Idaho

BOISE
Tropical Sunrise
Delsa's Ice Cream Parlor
7923 Ustick Rd.
(208) 375-3495

COEUR D'ALENE
*Help Me Make It (Through
the Night)*
I.C. Sweets
602 E. Sherman Ave.
(208) 664-1549

EAGLE
Brownie Sundae
State Street Ice Cream
Shoppe
257 E. State St.
(208) 938-6108

McCALL
Hot Fudge Sundae
McCall Drug & Gifts
1001 N. 2nd St.
(208) 634-2433

PLACERVILLE
Crème de Menthe Sundae
Sarsaparilla Ice Cream
Parlor
205 S. Main St.
(208) 392-4484
*nonalcoholic

TWIN FALLS
Blackberry Sundae
Crowley's Soda Fountain
& General Store
144 Main Ave. S. B.
(208) 733-1041

Illinois

BELLEVILLE
Copacabana
The White Cottage
102 Lebanon Ave.
(618) 234-1120

CHICAGO
S'More Sundae
Bobtail Soda Fountain
2951 N. Broadway
(773) 880-7372

*World's Smallest Hot
Fudge Sundae*
Ed Debevic's
640 N. Wells St.
(312) 664-1707

Fudge with the Works
George's Restaurant and
Ice Cream Parlor
3222-24 W. Foster Ave.
(773) 478-7707

Terrapin Sundae
Margie's Candies
1960 N. Western Ave.
(773) 384-1035

Banana Splice
Scooter's Frozen Custard
1658 W. Belmont Ave.
(773) 244-6415

War of the Worlds
Zephyr Ice Cream
Restaurant
1767 W. Wilson Ave.
(773) 728-6070

DOWNERS GROVE
Downers Delight
Every Day's a Sundae
990 Warren Ave.
(630) 810-9155

ELMHURST
Sour Cherry Sundae
Kopper Kitchen
Restaurant and Ice Cream
Parlor
601 W. St. Charles Rd.
(630) 834-2118

EVANSTON
Turtle Super Sundae
Evanston Creamery
1301 Chicago
(847) 328-3113

Evanston Express Sundae
Hartigan's Ice Cream
Shoppe
2909 Central St.
(847) 491-1232

FOREST PARK
*Adam's Hawaiian
Heaven*
The Brown Cow
7314 W. Madison St.
(708) 366-7970

HOMEWOOD
Hot Fudge Sundae
Mitchell's Candies & Ice
Cream
18211 Dixie Hwy.
(708) 799-3835

LANSING
Muddle Sundae
Gayety's Chocolates and
Ice Creams
3306 Ridge Rd.
(708) 418-0062

LEBANON
Maple Leaf Rag
Dr. Jazz Soda Fountain &
Grille
230 West St. Louis St.
(618) 537-2200

MARYVILLE
Caramel Apple Sundae
Bobby's Frozen Custard
2525 N. Center St.
(618) 345-3002

MOLINE
C'est Si Bon
Lagomarcino
Confectionery
1422 5th Ave.
(309) 764-1814

Dusty Road
Whitey's Ice Cream
2525 41st St.
(309) 762-2175

MOUNT PROSPECT
Girl Scout Cookie Sundae
Capannari Ice Cream
10 S. Pine
(847) 392-2277

OAK PARK
Hot Fudge Turtle

Petersen's Ice Cream
1100 Chicago Ave.
(708) 386-6131

PALOS PARK
Strawberry Sundae
Plush Horse Ice Cream
Parlor
12301 S. 86th Ave.
(708) 448-0550

SOUTH HOLLAND
Turtle Sundae
Cunis Candies
1030 E. 162nd St.
(708) 596-2440

SYCAMORE
Schwartz Sundae
Ollie's Frozen Custard
2290 Oakland Dr.
(815) 758-8222

WILMETTE
Pineapple Sundae
Homer's Homemade
Gourmet Ice Cream
1237 Green Bay Rd.
(847) 251-0477

Indiana

AVON
Cherry Sundae
Frost Bite
7025 Galen Dr. W.
(317) 272-2483

BRAZIL
Lemon Sundae
The Fountain at Lynn's
Pharmacy
22 W. National Ave.
(812) 446-2381

COLUMBUS
Hot Fudge Sundae
Zaharako's
329 Washington St.
(812) 379-9329

GEORGETOWN
*Upside Down Banana
Split*
Polly's Freeze
5242 State Rd. 62
(812) 945-6911

GREENWOOD
Mexican Sundae
Mrs. Curl Ice Cream Shop
259 S. Meridian St.
(317) 882-1031

INDIANAPOLIS
Hoosier Delight
Ritter's Frozen Custard
4840 W. 57th St.
(317) 293-1417

S'more Supreme
Sundae's Ice Cream
9922 E 79th St.
(317) 570-0533
MADISON

The Army Navy
Mundt's Candies
207 West Main St.
(812) 265-6171

SOUTH BEND
Four Horsemen
South Bend Chocolate
Café
122 South Michigan
(574) 287-0725

STARLIGHT
Three Acre Sundae
Joe Huber's Family Farm &
Restaurant
2421 Scottsville Rd.
(812) 923-5255

UPLAND
Turtle Sundae
Ivanhoe's Drive In
979 S. Main St.
(765) 998-7261

WEST LAFAYETTE
Blondie Sundae
Snowbear Frozen Custard
620 W. Stadium Ave.
(765) 743-8024

Iowa

BELLEVUE
Mississippi Gambler
Grandpa's Parlour
306 S. Riverview Dr.
(563) 872-4240

BETTENDORF
Sugar Daddy Dish

Happy Joe's Pizza & Ice
Cream Parlor
2430 Spruce Hills Dr.
(563) 359-5457

DAVENPORT
Happy Thought
Lagomarcino's
Confectionery
2132 E. 11th St.
(563) 324-6137

DENISON
*Chocolate Mint Marble
Sundae*
Reiney's Soda Fountain
1301 Broadway
(712) 263-4752

DES MOINES
Turtle Sundae
Bauder Pharmacy
3802 Ingersoll Ave.
(515) 255-1124

DUBUQUE
English Toffee Sundae
Betty Jane Homemade
Candies
3049 Asbury Rd.
(563) 582-4668

ELDORA
Cracker Jack Sundae
Ahoy Fountain
1266 Edgington Ave.
(641) 939-5881

FORT MADISON
Peach Sundae
Hall's Old Fashioned Ice
Cream
2002 Avenue L
(319) 372-7293

LE MARS
Goliath Sundae
Blue Bunny Ice Cream
Parlor
26 5th Ave. N.W.
(712) 546-4522

NORTH ENGLISH
Black Raspberry Sundae
E V Malt Shop
226 S. Main St.
(319) 664-3390

SIDNEY
Space Sundae

Penn Drug Co.
714 Illinois St.
(712) 374-2513

SIOUX CITY
Goshawful Gooey
Green Gables
1800 Pierce St.
(712) 258-4246

WILTON
The Wilton Special
Candy Kitchen
310 Cedar St.
(319) 732-2278

Kansas

ASHLAND
Hot Fudge Sundae
Fudge Man's Ice Cream
Shop
816 Main St.
(620) 635-2896

LAWRENCE
Suicide Squeeze
Sheridan's Frozen Custard
2030 W. 23rd St.
(785) 331-4426

*Hot Fudge Waffle Dish
Sundae*
Sylas & Maddy's Home
Made
1014 Massachusetts St.
(785) 832-8323

LEAVENWORTH
Banana Split
Corner Pharmacy
5th and Delaware
(913) 682-1602

TOPEKA
*Brown Bread Caramel
Sundae*
Potwin Drug
124 N.W. Fillmore
(785) 368-3888

WICHITA
Aspen Snowball
Old Mill Tasty Shop
604 E. Douglas Ave.
(316) 264-6500

Kentucky

LOUISVILLE
Brown Turtle Sundae
Dairy Kastle
575 Eastern Pkwy.
(502) 634-8990

Banana Split
Dizzy Whizz
217 West St. Catherine
(502) 583-3828

Hot Butterscotch Sundae
Homemade Ice Cream &
Pie Kitchen
2525 Bardstown Rd.
(502) 459-8184

BELLEVUE
Hawaiian Delight
Schneider's Sweet Shop
420 Fairchild Ave.
(859) 431-3545

Louisiana

BATON ROUGE
Cinnamon Apple Sundae
Calendar's Restaurant
11777 Coursey Blvd.
(225) 291-8175

LAFAYETTE
Banana Split
Borden's Ice Cream
1103 Jefferson
(337) 235-9291

NEW ORLEANS
Coppa Gelato Sundae
Angelo Brocato Ice Cream
214 N. Carrollton Ave.
(504) 486-1465

Tchoupoulas Sundae
Creole Creamery
4924 Prytania St.
(504) 894-8680

Peanut Butter Sundae
Sophie's
1912 Magazine St.
(504) 561-0291

SLIDELL
Banana Sundae
Old Town Slidell Soda Shop
301 Cousin St.
(985) 649-4806

Maine

DAMARISCOTTA
Blueberry Sundae
Round Top Ice Cream
526 Main St.
(207) 563-5307

FARMINGTON
Banana Split
Cold Farms Ice Cream
393 Main St.
(207) 778-3617

FREEPORT
Peanut Supreme Sundae
Classic Custard
150 US Route 1
(207) 865-4417

GRAY
Banana Split
Cole Farms
64 Lewiston Rd.
(207) 657-4714

PORTLAND
Hot Fudge Sundae
Beal's Old Fashioned Ice
Cream
12 Moulton St.
(207) 828-1335

SANFORD
Barn Roof
Shain's of Maine
1491 Main St. (Rt. 109 N.)
(207) 324-1449

SKOWHEGAN
Pot Hole Sundae
Gifford's Famous Ice
Cream
503 Madison Ave.
(207) 474-2257

Butterscotch Sundae
Carlton's Old Fashioned
Ice Cream
49 Water St.
(207) 882-6622

YORK BEACH
Hot Penuche Sundae
The Goldenrod
2 Railroad Ave.
(207) 363-2621

Maryland

ANNAPOLIS
Maple Walnut Sundae
Storm Bros. Ice Cream
Factory
130 Dock St.
(410) 263-3376

BALTIMORE
*Peanut Butter Fudge
Sundae*
Circle Drive-In Ice Cream
Co.
555 Dundalk Ave.
(443) 524-3610

The Bundt Blast
Lee's Ice Cream
301 Light St.
(& other locations)
(401) 727-8776

Brownie Sundae
Sylvan Beach Ice Cream
1405 Forge Ave.
(410) 433-6800

The Santa Maria
Vaccaro's Italian Pastry
Shop
222 Albemarle St.
(410) 685-4905

BETHESDA
The Old Glory Parfait
Gifford's Ice Cream &
Candy
7237 Woodmont Ave.
(301) 907-3436

BOWIE
Spaghetti Ice Sundae
Simple Pleasures Ice Caf
6948 Laurel-Bowie Rd.
(301) 809-5880

BRANDYWINE
*Hot Fudge Brownie
Sundae*
Ice Cream Factory & Café
13700 Old Brandywine Rd.
(301) 372-8782

EASTON
Candy Bar Sundae
Old Towne Creamery
9B Goldsborough St.
(410) 820-5223

ELLICOTT CITY
Mint Sundae
Old Fashioned Ice Cream
Shoppe
9150-17 Baltimore
National Pike
(410) 480-2856

OCEAN CITY
Dusty Dumser
Dumser's Dairyland Drive-In
12305 Coastal Hwy.
(410) 250-5543

Hall of Fame Banana Split
Kelly's Front Porch
1301 N. Atlantic Ave.
(410) 289-8134

Oceanbound Banana Yacht
Ice Cream Castle
12207 Coastal Hwy.
(& other location)
(410) 250-5003

ROCK HALL
Baby Ruth Sundae
Durding's Store
5742 Main St.
(410) 778-7957

ST. MICHAELS
Dusty Road
Justine's Ice Cream
106 N. Talbot St.
(410) 745-5416

TAKOMA PARK
The Volcano
Summer Delights
6939 Laurel Ave.
(301) 891-2880

TOWNSON
Poundcake Sundae
Moxley's
25 W. Allegheny Ave.
(410) 825-2544

Massachusetts

BOSTON
Quadruple Chocolate Sundae
Herrell's
15 Dunster St.
(617) 497-2179

DENNISPORT
Maple Walnut Sundae
Sundae School
381 Lower County Rd.
(508) 394-9122

DRACUT
Brownie Sundae
Shaw Farm
195 New Boston Rd.
(978) 957-0031

GRANBY
Chocolate Lover's Sundae
Cindy's Drive-In
455 East State St. (Route 202)
(413) 467-9866

HADLEY
Oreo Brownie Sundae
Pete's Drive-In
287 Russell St. (Route 9)
(413) 585-0241

HAVERHILL
Hot Apple Crisp Sundae
England's Microcreamery
109 Washington St.
(978) 373-6400

KINGSTON
Peanut Butter Sundae
Shorty's Ice Cream
54D Pembroke St. (Rt. 27)
(781) 585-3040

NEWTONVILLE
Belgian Waffle Sundae
Cabot's
743 Washington St.
(617) 964-9200

SHARON
Strawberry Shortcake Sundae
Crescent Ridge Dairy
355 Bay Rd.
(781) 784-2740

WALTHAM
Caramel Fudge Sundae
Lizzy's Ice Cream Parlor
367 Moody St.
(781) 893-6677

WESTFORD
Kimball Special
Kimball Farm

400 Littleton Rd.
(Rte. 110)
(978) 486-3891

WHITMAN
Fudgernutter
Peaceful Meadows Farm
60 Bedford St.
(781) 447-3889

VINEYARD HAVEN
Pig's Delight
Mad Martha's
20 Union St.
(508) 693-5883

Michigan

ANN ARBOR
Brownie Sundae
Stuchhi's
302 S. State St.
(734) 662-1700

BEULAH
Cherry Sundae
The Cherry Hut
(seasonal)
U.S. 31
(231) 882-4431

BEAVER ISLAND
Snicker Doodle Sundae
Beaver Island Lodge
38210 Beaver Lodge Dr.
(231-448-2396

COPPER HARBOR
Strawberry Sundae
Thimbleberry Shoppe
US-41 & M-26
(906) 289-4212

EAST GRAND RAPIDS
Almond Joy Sundae
Jersey Junction Ice Cream Parlor
652 Croswell Ave. S.E.
(616) 458-4107

FENNVILLE
Hot Fudge Donut Sundae
Crane's Pie Pantry
6054 124th Ave.
(269) 561-2297

HOLLAND
Tommy Turtle Sundae
Captain Sundae's
365 Douglas Ave.
(616) 396-5938

PENTWATER
Hokey-Pokey Sundae
Pentwater's House of
Flavors
210 S. Hancock St.
(231) 869-4009

ROYAL OAK
Hot Fudge Creampuff
Ray's Ice Cream Company
4233 Coolidge Hwy.
(248) 549-5256

ST. CLAIR SHORES
Hot Fudge Sundae
Stroh's
31359 Harper Ave.
(586) 294-2440

SAUGATUCK
Mount Baldhead Sundae
Saugatuck Drugstore
201 Butler St.
(269) 857-2300

SOUTH HAVEN
Pig's Dinner Sundae
Sherman's Dairy Bar
1601 Phoenix Rd.
(269) 637-8251

TECUMSEH
Tin Roof
The Chocolate Vault
110-116 W. Chicago Blvd.
(517) 423-7602

TRAVERSE CITY
Udder Delight
Moomer's Homemade Ice
Cream
7263 N. Long Lake Rd.
(231) 941-4122

Minnesota

AFTON
Hot Turtle Sundae
Selma's Ice Cream Parlor
3419 Saint Croix Trail S.
(651) 436-8067

DULUTH
Inside-Out Sundae
The Green Mill
340 S. Lake Ave.
(218) 727-7000

EXCELSIOR
Caramel Apple Sundae
Adele's Frozen Custard
800 Excelsior Blvd.
(952) 470-0035

MINNEAPOLIS
Hot Fudge Sundae
Edina Creamery
5055 France Ave. S.
(612) 920-2169

Mocha Sundae
The Pumphouse
Creamery
4754 Chicago Ave. S.
(612) 825-2021

Talking Oreo
Sebastian Joe's Ice Cream
Café
1007 W Franklin Ave.
(612) 870-0065

ST. PAUL
Banana Split
Izzy's Ice Cream Café
2034 Marshall Ave.
(651) 603-1458

Tin Roof
Sunday's Ice Cream
2100 Snelling Ave. N.
(651) 639-1051

Mississippi

BRANDON
Hot Fudge Sundae
Always Sundae
5649 Hwy. 25
(601) 919-1144

HATTIESBURG
Banana Royale
Walnut Square Pharmacy
124 Walnut St.
(601) 543-0111

HERNANDO
Sweetheart Sundae

Velvet Cream
2290 Highway 51 S.
(662) 429-6540

OXFORD
Hot Caramel Sundae
Chaney's Pharmacy
501 Bramlett Blvd.
(662) 234-7221

Pineapple Sundae
Sno Biz
1707 University Ave.
(662) 234-8889

TUSCALOOSA
Tuscaloosa Turtle
Papa's College Custard
9710 Highway 69 S.
(205) 759-8076

WAVELAND
Chocolate Sundae
Waveland Pharmacy
112 Auderer Blvd.
(228) 463-1055

Missouri

BLUE SPRINGS
*Black & White Sundae aka
Referee Sundae*
Custard's Last Stand
1950 N.W. 7 Hwy.
(816) 220-1957

FLORISSANT
Turtle Sundae
Fritz's Frozen Custard
1055 Saint Catherine St.
(314) 839-4100

HANNIBAL
Jumpin' Frog
Main Street Soda Fountain
207 South Main St.
(573) 248-1295

INDEPENDENCE
Harry Truman Sundae
Clinton's Drugstore
100 W. Maple Ave.
(816) 833-2625

JEFFERSON CITY
Rock & Roll Sundae
Central Dairy
610 Madison St.
(573) 635-6148

JOPLIN
The Bopper
Shake's Frozen Custard
1441 S. Rangeline Rd.
(417) 782-6997

KANSAS CITY
Turtle Creek Sundae
Foo's Fabulous Frozen
Custard
6235 Brookside Blvd.
(816) 523-2520

Cookie Monster Sundae
Murray's Ice Creams &
Cookies
4120 Pennsylvania Ave.
(816) 931-5646

ST. LOUIS
Crown Sundae
Crown Candy Kitchen
1401 St. Louis Ave.
(314) 621-9650

*Chocolate Heaven
Sundae*
Serendipity Homemade
Ice Cream
8130 Big Bend Blvd.
(314) 962-2700

Sin Sunday
Ted Drewes Frozen
Custard
6726 Chippewa
(314) 481-2652

The Wizard
Mr. Wizard's Frozen
Custard
2101 S. Big Bend Blvd.
(314) 781-7566

Montana

BIG TIMBER
Big Timber Sundae
Cole Drug
136 McLeod
(406) 932-5316

CONRAD
Marshmallow Sundae
Olson's Drug
5 Fourth Ave.
(406) 278-3261

ENNIS
*Chocolate Covered
Cherry Sundae*
Yesterday's Soda Fountain
at Ennis Pharmacy
124 Main St.
(406) 682-4246

GREAT FALLS
Brown Cow Sundae
Snyder Drug
2515 Sixth Ave. N.
(406) 452-6461

HELENA
Caramel Cashew Sundae
The Parrot Confectionery
42 N. Last Chance Gulch
(406) 442-1470

SUPERIOR
Chocolate Nut Sundae
Superior Drugstore
105 Mullan Rd. E.
(406) 822-4242

WEST YELLOWSTONE
Chocolate Sundae
Eagle's Store
3 Canyon St.
(406) 646-9300

Nebraska

ATKINSON
Haystack Sundae
R.F. Goeke Variety and
Old Fashioned
Soda Fountain
110 S. Main St.
(402) 925-2263

FREMONT
Butter Pecan Sundae
Sweete Shoppe
1149 E. 4th St.
(402) 721-7680

HOOPER
Pineapple Sundae
Ice Cream Parlor
207 W. Howard St.
(402) 654-3415

LINCOLN
Black Forest Sundae
University of Nebraska
Dairy Store

114 Food Industry Building
(402) 472-2828

LOUISVILLE
Cherry Sundae
Blake's Soda Fountain
213 Main St.
(402) 234-4095

OMAHA
Apple Spice Sundae
Ted & Wally's Ice Cream
1120 Jackson St.
(402) 341-5827

SCOTTSBLUFF
Strawberry Sundae
Platte Valley Creamery
1005 E. Overland
(308) 632-4225

SPRINGFIELD
Husker '61 Sundae
Springfield Drug
205 Main St.
(402) 253-2000

Nevada

ELY
Chocolate Sundae
Steptoe Drug
504 Aultman St.
(775) 289-2671

LAS VEGAS
Western Special
Luv-It Frozen Custard
505 E. Oakey Blvd.
(702) 384-6452

The Mudslide
Pyramid Ice Cream
3900 Las Vegas Blvd. S.
(702) 597-5330

VIRGINIA CITY
Hot Caramel Sundae
Red's Old-Fashioned
Candies
68 South C St.
(775) 847-0404

New Hampshire

BELMONT
Belly Buster
Jordan's Ice Creamery
Rural Route 106
(603) 267-1900

CONCORD
Danish Cone Sundae
Arnie's Place
164 Loudon Rd.
(603) 228-3225

DERRY
Strawberry Shortcake Sundae
Moo's Place Homemade
Ice Cream
27 Crystal Ave.
(603) 425-0100

KEENE
Fruit Salad Sundae
Rick's Gourmet Ice
Cream
149 Emerald St.
(603) 352-4226

LITTLETON
Sundae Dream Cone
Bishop's Homemade Ice
Cream
183 Cottage St.
(603) 444-6039

MANCHESTER
Fried Dough Sundae
Blake's Creamery
46 Milford St.
(603) 623-7242

PITTSFIELD
Apple Crisp Sundae
Appleview Orchard
1266 Upper City Rd.
(603) 435-6483

PORTSMOUTH
Hot Fudge Sundae
Annabelle's Natural Ice
Cream
49 Ceres St.
(603) 436-3400

WINDHAM
Strawberry Sundae
Johnson's Highland View
Farm

101 Range Rd.
(603) 898-3831

WOLFEBORO
Snow White Sundae
Bailey's Bubble
Railroad Ave.
(603) 569-3612

New Jersey

AVON BY THE SEA
Fudge Brownie Pie Sundae
Schneider's Restaurant
801 Main St.
(732) 775-1265

BEACH HAVEN
Phantom of the Opera
Show Place Ice Cream
Parlor
202 Centre St.
(609) 492-0018

BLOOMFIELD
American Beauty
Holstein's Brookdale
Confectionery
1063 Broad St.
(973) 338-7091

CAPE MAY
Red Raspberry Sundae
Rainbow Ice Cream Palace
Bayshore & Townbank
(609) 886-9891

ENGLEWOOD
Hot Fudge Sundae
Baumgart's Café
45 E. Palisade Ave.
(201) 569-6267

GREEN CREEK
Caramel Sundae
Little Danny's Ice Cream
(seasonal)
State Highway 47 N.
(609) 889-1139

HAZLET
"Nuts About You" Sundae
Temptation Ice Cream
Store
3091 Route 35
(732) 888-0999

HIGHLAND PARK
Bittersweet Chocolate Sundae

Corner Confectionery
248 Raritan Ave.
(732) 246-7373

LAVALETTE
Old Faithful
The Music Man
2305 Grand Central Ave.
(732) 854-2779

OCEAN CITY
Boardwalk Sundae
Tory's Ice Cream Parlour
3308 Asbury Ave.
(609) 391-7933

OCEAN GROVE
Brownie Sundae
Nagle's Apothecary Café
43 Main Ave.
(732) 776-9797

RIVERTON
The Train Wreck
Nelly Bly's Olde Tyme Ice
Cream Parlour
529 Main St.
(856) 303-0707

SPRING LAKE
Apple Crisp Sundae
Susan Murphy's
Homemade Ice Cream
601 Warren Ave.
(732) 449-1130

STONE HARBOR
C.M.P.
Springer's Homemade Ice
Cream
9420 3rd Ave.
(609) 368-4631

TOMS RIVER
Suicide Sundae
Mrs. Walker's Ice Cream
Parlor
908 Fisher Blvd.
(732) 506-0043

Hot Butterscotch Sundae
Sundaes
324 Route 166
(732) 349-6556

UPPER MONTCLAIR
The Farm
Applegate Farm
616 Grove St.
(973) 744-5900

WILDWOOD
Brownie Delight
Hassles Ice Cream Parlor
430 E. 20th Ave.
(609) 522-6191

New Mexico

ALBUQUERQUE
Cherry Sundae
Model Pharmacy
3636 Monte Vista Blvd.
N.E.
(505) 255-8686

Hot Fudge Sundae
Romero Street Ice Cream
Parlor
205 Romero St. N.W.
(505) 247-0221

LAS CRUCES
Green Chile Sundae
Caliche's Frozen Custard
590 South Valley Dr.
(505) 521-1161

LAS VEGAS
Banana Split
Plaza Drugs
178 Bridge St.
(505) 425-5221

SANTA FE
Banana Split
Delectables
720 Saint Michaels Dr.
(505) 438-8152

New York

BUFFALO
Iditarod Sundae
Anderson's Frozen
Custard
2634 Delaware Ave.
(716) 873-5330

The Brain Freeze
Condrell's Candies & Ice
Cream Parlor
2805 Delaware Ave.
(716) 877-4485

Strawberry Parfait
Parkside Candy
3208 Main St.
(716) 833-7540

EAST HAMPTON
Black Cherry Sundae
Scoop du Jour
35 Newtown Lane
(631) 329-4883

HYDE PARK
*One Free Hour in the
Candy Store*
Eveready Diner
540 Albany Post Rd.
(845 229-8100)

ITHACA
Maple Syrup Sundae
Cornell Dairy Bar
Stocking Hall
Tower Road
(607) 255-3272

Nuttin' Honey Sundae
Purity Ice Cream
700 Cascadilla St. (at
Route 13)
(607) 272-1545

NEW YORK
The Hot Fudge Sundae
Brooklyn Diner USA
212 W 57 St.
Manhattan
(212) 977-1957

Hot Fudge Sundae
Eddie's Sweet Shop
105-29 Metropolitan Ave.
Forest Hills/Queens
(718) 520-8514

Kitchen Sink
Jahn's
11703 Hillside Ave.
Richmond Hill/Queens
(718) 724-2120

Hot Butterscotch Sundae
Mary's Dairy
171 W. Fourth St.
Manhattan
(212) 242-6874

Death by Peanut Butter
Peanut Butter & Co.
240 Sullivan St.
Manhattan
(212) 677-3995

Brooklyn Bridge
Uncle Louis G

1361 Coney Island Ave.
Brooklyn (plus 16 others)
(718) 724-2120

*Forbidden Broadway
Sundae*
Serendipity 3
225 E. 60th St.
Manhattan
(212) 838-3531

Shockapalooza
Shake Shack
in Madison Square Park
(Madison at 23rd St.)
Manhattan
(212) 889-6600

OXFORD
P, B & J Sundae
Hoppie's Ice Cream
2 Lafayette Park
(607) 843-2663

PORT JERVIS
*Deep Fried Ice Cream
Sundae*
Riverside Creamery
5 Water St.
(845) 856-8560

RIVERHEAD
Pecan Treat Sundae
Snow Flake Ice Cream
Shoppe
1152 West Main St.
(631) 727-4394

ROCHESTER
*Chocolate Chip Cookie
Sundae*
Corky's
1136 Monroe Ave.
(585) 461-4159

Sandy Beach Sundae
Read's Ice Cream
3208 Latta Rd.
(716) 227-8650

SYLVAN BEACH
Maple Nut Blast
Cinderella's Cafe
1208 Main St.
(315) 762-4280

Mexican Sundae
Eddie's
901 Main St.
(315) 762-5430

WYANSTSKILL
Hot Fudge Brownie
Sundae
Moxie's Ice Cream
1344 Spring Ave.
(518) 283-4901

SLINGERLANDS
Toasted Donut Delight
Toll Gate Ice Cream &
Coffee Shop
1569 New Scotland Rd.
(518) 439-9824

TARRYTOWN
What-a-Lotta-Sundae
Main Street Sweets
35 Main St.
(914) 332-5757

TRUMANSBURG
Cayuga-uga Sundae
Cayuga Lake Creamery
8421 Rt. 89
(607) 387-3108

North Carolina

CONOVER
Cow Chip Sundae
Udderly Delicious Ice
Cream
1006 Conover Blvd. W.
(828) 465-1070

CHARLOTTE
Hot Fudge Sundae
Carolina Creamery
11300 Lawyers Rd.
(704) 545-0401

GASTONIA
Chocolate Nut Sundae
Tony's Ice Cream
520 E. Franklin Blvd.
(704) 853-0018

LINCOLNTON
The Minty Grasshopper
Morgan's Dairy Bar
1619 E. Main St.
(704) 748-2599

MANTEO
Wipe Out
Big Al's Soda Fountain and
Grill
100 Patty Lane
(Hwy 64/264)
(252) 473-5570

North Dakota

FARGO
Dakota Frozen Earth
Zandbroz Variety
420 N. Broadway
(701) 239-4729

GRAFTON
Cherry Sundae
Ice Box
120 E. 12th St.
(701) 352-0087

JAMESTOWN
Dusty Road Sundae
Polar King
621 13th Ave., S.E.
(701) 251-1585

KENMARE
Turtle Sundae
Chill-N-Grill
515 6th St., N.E.
(701) 385-4370

MANDAN
Buffalo Nut Sundae
Mandan Drug and Soda
Fountain
316 W. Main St.
(701) 663-5900

STANLEY
Banana Split
Dakota Drug Co.
118 Main St.
(701) 628-2255

WATFORD CITY
The Twister
Twist Drive-In
404 2nd Ave., S.W.
(701) 842-3595

Ohio

AKRON
The Kitchen Sink
Taggarts Ice Cream Parlor
1401 Fulton Rd., N.W.
(330) 452-6844

CINCINNATI
Bourbon Street
Aglamesis Brothers
3046 Madison Rd.
(513) 531-5196

Banana Split
Putz's Creamy Whip
2673 Putz Pl.
(513) 681-8668

Turtle Waffle Dish
Zip Dip Creamery Whip
4050 Drew Ave.
(513) 574-6252

CIRCLEVILLE
Buckeye Sundae
Wittich's Candy Shop
117 W. High St.
(740) 474-3313

CLEVELAND
Scotch and Fudge
Tremont Scoops
2362 Professor St.
(216) 781-0352

COLUMBUS
Strawberry Sundae
Denise's Homemade Ice
Cream
2899 N. High St.
(614) 267-8800

Blondie Sundae
Handel's Homemade Ice
Cream
6820 Refugee Rd.
(614) 920-9409

GARNETT
Vanilla Sundae
Yesterday's Soda Fountain
& Café
122 East Fifth Avenue
(785) 448-6961

LAKEWOOD
Sweet William
Malley's Chocolates
14822 Madison Ave.
(216) 529-6262

LEBANON
Lebanon Sundae
Village Ice Cream Parlor
22 S. Broadway St.
(513) 932-6918

MEDINA
The Gut Buster
Elm Farm's "Once Upon a
Sundae" Ice Cream Parlor
1050 Lafayette Rd.
(330) 722-3839

REYNOLDSBURG
Tin Roof
Johnson's Real Ice Cream
7111 E. Main St.
(614) 577-1916

TOLEDO
Turtle Sundae
Famous Amy's Drive-In
2820 N. Summit St.
(419) 729-2601

UTICA
Buckeye Sundae
Velvet Ice Cream
11324 Mount Vernon Rd.
(740) 892-3921

VERMILION
Teddy Bear Sundae
Ednamae's
5598 Liberty Ave.
(216) 409-8361

WEST CHESTER
Coconut Macaroon Sundae
The Cone
6855 Tylersville Rd.
(513) 779-7040

WESTERVILLE
Fudge Brownie Sundae
Knight's Ice Cream
596 South Cleveland Ave.
(614) 890-2353

WESTLAKE
Cleveland Brownie
Mitchell's Homemade
26161 Detroit Rd.
(440) 250-0952

WILMINGTON
Banana Split
Gibson's Goodies
718 Ohio Ave.
(937) 383-2373

WOOSTER
Cow Pie Sundae
Hartzler Ice Cream Shoppe
5454 Cleveland Rd.
(330) 345-8190

YELLOW SPRINGS
King Kong Banana Split
Young's Jersey Dairy

6880 Springfield-Xenia Rd.
(937) 325-0629

ZANESVILLE
Tin Roof Sundae
Tom's Ice Cream Bowl
532 McIntire Ave.
(740) 452-5267

Oklahoma

BOISE CITY
Smiley Face Sundae
Ice Cream Parlor
500 E. Main St.
(580) 544-2872

OKLAHOMA CITY
Peanut Butter Hot Fudge Sundae
Braum's Ice Cream & Dairy Stores
1204 N.W. 17th St.
(405) 521-1598

The Be-Here-Now'm Banana Split
Grateful Bean Café
1039 N. Walker Ave.
(405) 236-3503

TULSA
Sooner Spooner
Freckles Frozen Custard
9607 E. 71st Street
(918) 252-2663

Oregon

ASHLAND
Much Ado About Fudge
Lithia Fountain & Grill
303 East Main
(541) 488-0179

BEND
Turtle Sundae
Goody's Soda Fountain
957 N.W. Wall St.
(541) 389-5185

BROOKINGS
Hanna Banana Slug Split
Slugs 'n Stones Ice Cream Cones
16360 Lower Harbor Rd.
(541) 469-7584

EUGENE
Euphoria Hot Fudge Sundae
Prince Puckler's Ice Cream
1605 E. 19th Ave.
(541) 344-4418

HOOD RIVER
Screaming Brownie Sundae
Mike's Ice Cream
504 Oak St.
(541) 386-6260

INDEPENDENCE
Black and White Sundae
Taylor's Ice Cream Fountain
296 S. Main St.
(503) 838-1124

LAKE OSWEGO
Strawberry Shortcake Sundae
Tillamook Ice Creamery and Restaurant
37 A Ave.
(503) 636-4933

SEASIDE
Lewis and Clark
Zinger's Ice Cream Parlor
210 Broadway
(503) 738-3939

Pennsylvania

BALLY
Longacre Special
Longacre's Modern Dairy Bar
1445 Route 100
(610) 845-7551

CANONSBURG
Hot Fudge Sundae
Sarris Candies
511 Adams Ave.
(724) 745-4042

CHAMBERSBURG
Marshmallow Mess
Olympia Candy Kitchen
43 South Main St.
(717) 263-3282

FRACKVILLE
Atomic Banana Split
Dutch Kitchen
Restaurant
433 S. Lehigh Ave.
(570) 874-3265

LATROBE
Banana Split
Valley Dairy
1914 Ligonier St.
(724) 539-0901

LEWISBERRY
C.M.P.
Reeser's Soft Ice Cream
880 Old Rossville Road
(717) 938-1781

MANHEIM
Double Diamond Sundae
Kreider Farms
1461 Lancaster Road,
Route 72
(717) 665-5039

MOUNT POCONO
*Three Stooges Banana
Split*
Village Malt Shoppe at
Casino Theatre
110 Rte. 611
(570) 839-7831

NEWTOWN
Night & Day
Goodnoe Farm
298 N. Sycamore St.
(215) 968-3875

NORTH HUNTINGTON
Wet Walnut Sundae
Kerber's Dairy
1856 Guffey Rd.
(724) 863-6930

OAKMONT
*French Fried Ice Cream
Sundae*
Hoffstot's Café Monaco
533 Allegheny Ave.
(412) 828-8555

PHILADELPHIA
Flutter-Nutter
Bredenbeck's Bakery
8126 Germantown Ave.
(215) 247-7374

Southern Sympathizer
The Franklin Fountain
116 Market St.

(215) 627-1899
The Ooey Gooey
Scoop DeVille
1734 Chestnut St.
(215) 988-9992

PITTSBURGH
Flood of '36 Sundae
Klavon's Ice Cream Parlor
2801 Penn Ave.
(412) 434-0451

SOUTH TAMAQUA
Original Atomic Sundae
Leiby's Ice Cream House
848 West Penn Pike
(570) 386-4389

YORK
Monkey in the Middle
Mack's Ice Cream
2731 S. Queen St.
(717) 741-2027

SPRINGDALE
Blue Moon Sundae
Glen's Frozen Custard
400 Pittsburgh St.
(724) 274-5516

Rhode Island

CUMBERLAND
Diamond Hill Sundae
Ice Cream Machine
4288 Diamond Hill Rd.
Cumberland
(401) 333-5053

NARRAGANSETT
Hot Fudge Sundae
Brickley's Ice Cream
921 Boston Neck Rd.
(401) 789-1784

PROVIDENCE
Elephant's Memory
Maxmillian's Ice Cream
Café
1074 Hope St.
(401) 273-7230

Brookie Sundae
Newport Creamery
673 Smith St.
(401) 351-4677

RUMFORD
The Sunshine Sundae

Sunshine Creamery
305 N. Broadway
(401) 431-2828

SOMERSET
Banana Split
Somerset Creamery
1931 Grand Army Hwy.
(508) 672-5510

TIVERTON
Mixed Fruit Sundae
Gray's Ice Cream
16 East Rd .
(401) 624-4500

WARREN
Strawberry Sundae
Delekta's Pharmacy
496 Main St.
(401) 245-6767

South Carolina

EASLEY
Nut Sundae
Easley Ice Cream Parlor
136 E. Main St.
(864) 859-9186

HILTON HEAD
Build-Your-Own Sundae
Hilton Head Ice Cream
55 New Orleans Rd.
(843) 842-6333

MYRTLE BEACH
Oreo Sundae
Kirk's 1890 Ice Cream
Parlor
2500 N. Kings Hwy.
(843) 626-3422

Vanna Banana Sundae
Original Painter's
Homemade Ice Cream
2408 Hwy. 17 S.
(843) 272-6934

SUMMERVILLE
Pig's Trough Sundae
Ye Ole Fashioned Ice
Cream
602 Old Trolley Rd.
(843) 871-7859

South Dakota

ELK POINT
Guilty Conscience
Edgar's at Pioneer Drug
107 E. Main St.
(605) 356-3336

MITCHELL
Chocolate Sundae
Olde Ice Cream Shoppe
605 N Main St.
(605) 995-1356

HILL CITY
Brownie Blast Sundae
Pauline's Ice Cream
Parlour & Sweet Shop
357 Main St.
(605) 574-2423

RAPID CITY
Tyler's Turtle
Armadillo Ice Cream
Shoppe
202 Main St.
(605) 355-0507

Tennessee

CHATANOOGA
Wet Walnut Sundae
Clumpies Ice Cream
Company
26-B Frazier Ave. (at
Coolidge Park)
(423) 267-5425

LOUDON
Banana Split
Tic-Toc Ice Cream Parlor
504 Grove St.
(865) 408-9867

NASHVILLE
Hot Fudge Sundae
Bobbie's Dairy Dip
5301 Charlotte Ave.
(615) 292-2112

Hot Butterscotch Sundae
Elliston Place Soda Shop
2111 Elliston Place
(615) 327-1090

SEVIERVILLE
Hot Caramel Sundae
The Creamery
230 Apple Valley Rd.
(865) 429-4113

Texas

AUSTIN
Texas Pineapple Sundae
Nau's Enfield Drug
1115 W Lynn St.
(512) 476-1221

DALLAS
Harry's Favorite Sundae
Wild About Harry's
3113 Knox St.
(214) 520-3113

DUBLIN
Sundae with the Works
Old Doc's Soda Shop
105 E. Elm
(888) 398-1024

EL PASO
Banana Split
San Pedro Thrifty
Pharmacy
3712 Alameda Ave.
(915) 533-8446

GALVESTON
Chocolate Sundae
La King's Confectionery
2323 Strand
(409) 762-6100

GRANBURY
Texas-Size Banana Split
Rinky Tink's Sandwich
Shop and Ice Cream Parlor
108 North Houston St.
(817) 573-4323

GRAPEVINE
The Ritzy Splitzy
Ritzy's
2225 E. Grapeville Mills
Circle
(972) 691-1113

HOUSTON
Sundae-on-a-Cone
Hank's Ice Cream Parlor
9291 Main St.
(713) 665-5103

*Death by Chocolate
Sundae*
Oscar's Creamery
13837 Breck St.
(281) 880-9007

WATAUGA
Royal Turtle Sundae
Sheridan's Frozen Custard
7428 Denton Hwy.
(817) 514-7437

Utah

BINGHAM CITY
Banana Split
Idle Isle
24 S. Main St.
(435) 734-2468

LOGAN
Double Devil Sundae
Bluebird Restaurant
19 N. Main St.
(435) 752-3155

OREM
*Peanut Butter Burst
Sundae*

Coney's Frozen Custard
242 E. University Parkway
(801) 371-0500

RICHMOND
Casco Nut Sundae
Casper's Retail Malt
Shoppe
11805 North 200 E.
(435) 258-2477

SALT LAKE CITY
Hot Fudge Brownie
Hires Big H
425 South 700 E.
(801) 364-4582

The Jazz
Squirrel Brothers Ice
Cream
605 East 400 S.
(801) 359-4207

Vermont

BARRE
Brownie Sundae
Strafford Organic
Creamery
at the Farmer's Diner
240 N. Main St.
(802) 476-7623

BENNINGTON
Blueberry Sundae
Northside Dairy Bar
217 Northside Dr.
(802) 442-5644

EAST MONTEPELIER
Maple Sundae
Bragg Farm Sugarhouse
1005 Vermont
(802) 223-5757

LYNDONVILLE
Pineapple Sundae
Carmen's Ice Cream
1000 Broad
(802) 626-1174

MANCHESTER
Hot Fudge Sundae
Mother Myrick's
Confectionery & Ice
Cream Parlor
Historic Route 7A
(802) 362-1560

Virginia

ALEXANDRIA
Door County Sour
Del Ray Dreamery
2310 Mount Vernon Ave.
(703) 683-7767

ARLINGTON
Hot Fudge Sundae
Lazy Sundae
2925 Wilson Blvd.
(703) 525-4960

CHINCOTEAGUE
Hot Apple Sundae
Mister Whippy
6201 Maddox Blvd.
(757) 336-5122

FRONT ROYAL
Caramel Cashew Sundae
Spelunker's Frozen
Custard
116 South St.
(540) 631-0300

GREAT FALLS
Brownie Sundae
Thelma's Country Store
10200 Colvin Run Rd.
(703) 757-2800

MANASSAS
Pecan Turtle Delight
Kline's Freeze
8200 Centreville Road
(703) 368-2013

NORFOLK
Co-ed Sundae
Doumar's
1919 Monticello Ave.
(757) 627-4163

RESTON
Baker's Blitz
Lee's Ice Cream
11917 Freedom Dr.
(703) 471-8902

WINCHESTER
The Peanut Thing
Da Da's
29 Weems Lane
(540) 678-4289

VIENNA
Strawberry Sundae
Nielsen's Frozen Custard
144 Church St., N.W.
(703) 255-5553

Washington

BELLINGHAM
Bomb Sundae
Mallard Ice Cream
1323 Railroad Ave.
(360) 734-3884

The Viking Bowl
The Malt Shop
1135 Railroad Ave.
(360) 676-5156

OCEAN SHORES
The Murphy's Sundae Special
Murphy's Candy & Ice
Cream
172 W. Chance A La Mer
N.W.
(360) 289-0927

PORT TOWNSEND
Hot Fudge Sundae
Elevated Ice Cream
627 Water St.
(360) 385-1156

PULLMAN
Espresso Sundae
Ferdinand's Ice Cream
Shoppe
S. Fairway Drive
Washington State
University
(509) 335-2141

SEATTLE
Jet City Buzz
Mix Ice Cream Bar
4507 University Way N.E.
(206) 547-3436

SNOHOMISH
Black and White Sundae
Snohomish Valley Ice
Cream & Candy Co.
902 First St.
(360) 568-1133

SPOKANE
Native Huckleberry Sundae
Mary Lou's Milk Bottle
802 W. Garland Ave.
(509) 325-1772

YAKIMA
Banana Split
Museum Soda Fountain
2105 Tieton Dr.
(509) 248-0747

West Virginia

CHARLESTON
Butterscotch Sundae
Blossom Deli & Soda
Fountain
904 Quarrier St.
(304) 345-2233

Espresso Sundae
Ellen's Homemade Ice
Cream
225 Capitol St.
(304) 343-6488

Cherry Sundae
Marquis Gourmet Ice
Cream
3001 Charleston Town
Center
(304) 344-1421

KANAWHA CITY
Strawberry Sundae
Trivillian's Pharmacy
215 35th St., S.E.
(304) 343-8621

MARTINSBURG
Jo-Jo Sundae
Patterson's Old Fashion
Drugstore
134 S. Queen St.
(304) 267-8903

Wisconsin

CEDARBURG
The Oh Fudge!
The Chocolate Factory
W62 N577 Washington
Ave.
(262) 377-8877

LA CROSSE
Lacrosse Special
The Sweet Shop
1113 Caledonia St.
(608) 784-7724

MADISON
*Grilled Pound Cake Hot
Fudge Sundae*
Ella's Deli & Ice Cream
Parlor
2902 E. Washington Ave.
(608) 241-5291
Death by Chocolate
Michael's Frozen Custard
2531 Monroe St.
(608) 231-3500

MANITOWOC
High School Special
Beernsten's
108 North Eighth St.
(414) 684-9616

MILWAUKEE
Fat Cat Sundae
Bella's Fat Cat
1233 E. Brady St.
(414) 273-2113

Zombie
Gilles Frozen Custard
7515 West Bluemound Rd.
(414) 453-4875

S'mores Sundae
Kopp's Frozen Custard
Stand
5373 N. Port Washington
Rd.
(414) 961-2006

Dusty Trail
Leon's Frozen Custard
3131 S. 27th St.
(414) 383-1784

Oreo of My Heart
Lixx
2597 N. Downer Ave.
(414) 332-3338

Peanut Butter Cup
Oscar's Frozen Custard
2362 S. 108th St.
(414) 327-5220

OSHKOSH
Mudslide Sundae
Leon's Frozen Custard
121 W. Murdock Ave.
(920) 231-7755

WALES
Armadillo Sundae
Le Duc's Frozen Custard
240 W. Summit Ave.
(262) 968-2894

WATERTOWN
Bigger Than Bill
Mullen's Dairy Bar
212 W. Main St.
(920) 261-4278

WHITEWATER
The Ice Berg
Shiver's
University of Wisconsin
University Center
(262) 472-1161

Wyoming

CHUGWATER
Chocolate Sundae
Chugwater Soda Fountain
314 First St.
(307) 422-3222

BUFFALO
The Polish Sundae
Ice Cream Shop
665 E. Hart St.
(307) 684-7347

GILETTE
Hot Fudge Sundae
Ice Cream Land
802 E. 3rd St.
(307) 685-0550

LARAMIE
Brownie Delight
Gramma's Olde Ice
Cream Parlor
1657 Snowy Range Rd.
(307) 742-3194

SHOSHONI
Pina Colada Sundae
Yellowstone Drugstore
127 Main St.
(307) 876-2539

THAYNE
Huckleberry Sundae
Lower Valley United Drug
& Soda Fountain
190 S. Main St.
(307) 883-4600